The Book in America

Books in the Library of Congress Classics series
from Fulcrum Publishing

America's Botanical Beauty

Americans on the Move

The Book in America

Celebration of American Food

The First Americans

Gentle Conquest

Invention in America

The Library of Congress

Mapping the Civil War

Prints of the West

In addition:

Jefferson the Man

Civil War Maps

The Book in America

with Images from the Library of Congress

Richard W. Clement

Foreword by James H. Billington, The Librarian of Congress
Afterword by John Y. Cole, The Center for the Book

Published in cooperation with the Library of Congress

Fulcrum Publishing
Golden, Colorado

Library of Congress Cataloging-in-Publication Data
Clement, Richard W.
    The book in America / Richard W. Clement; with images from the Li-
brary of Congress.
        p.   cm.
    Includes bibliographical references and index.
    ISBN 1-55591-234-6 (hardcover)
    1. Books—United States—History. 2. Library of Congress.
I. Title.
Z8.U62C58 1996
002'.0974—dc20   96-10572
                                                                 CIP

Printed by Sung In Printing Company, Seoul, Korea
            0 9 8 7 6 5 4 3 2 1

Fulcrum Publishing
350 Indiana Street, Suite 350
Golden, Colorado 80401-5093
(800) 992-2908 • (303) 277-1623

To Susanne

Table of Contents

Foreword

In this ninth volume in the Library of Congress Classics series, Richard W. Clement, associate special collections librarian at the Kenneth Spencer Research Library, University of Kansas, presents an enlightening overview of *The Book in America*. Solidly documented and laced with anecdotes, this history of the book and its impact on our nation—from the arrival of the first volumes and early printing presses on the shores of the New World to current trends in publishing—amply demonstrates the crucial roles books have always played in the development of the American republic.

You will encounter in this volume editors, printers, publishers, and writers who have helped determine the direction of American publishing, and you will see how their foibles and prejudices—and their dedication to disseminating ideas and information—have contributed to a nation that has always ranked among the most literate in the world. The people who founded this country—including printer and publisher Ben Franklin—drew upon the ideas communicated to them through books. They, in turn, communicated their own revolutionary ideas through newspapers, books, and broadsides to a population ready to grapple with those ideas and upon whose collective wisdom the success of American democracy ultimately depended. One of the founding fathers, Thomas Jefferson, became, in later years, the principal founder of the world's largest and most eclectic library—the Library of Congress.

Since 1815, when Congress acquired Jefferson's personal library, the finest in America at the time, the Library of Congress book collection has expanded into the largest such collection in the world, numbering more than 25 million volumes—almost a quarter of the 110 million items in our overall holdings. The Library's Jefferson Building, opened in 1897 (and renovated and reopened in its centennial year), is a Temple of the Book; its iconography, murals, and works of art are a permanent tribute to the printed word. And, as John Y. Cole explains in his afterword, the Library is the home of the Center for the Book—a unique office devoted to the advocacy and study of books, reading, and the printed word.

The Library celebrates, preserves, and makes available the ideas, the creativity, the intellectual heritage given to us through books—even as we enter the electronic age with our National Digital Library initiative and our presence on the Internet. It is particularly fitting that the story of *The Book in America* be included in the Library of Congress Classics series. As Professor Clement makes abundantly clear in his narrative, the book is a resilient and adaptable medium of communication. It has been with us for two thousand years; we expect it will be with us, complementing the new electronic developments, for at least two thousand more.

James H. Billington
The Librarian of Congress

The Book in America

Introduction

cannot live without books." With this statement, addressed to John Adams, Thomas Jefferson voiced a national cultural truth. Jefferson understood that books are the threads from which the fabric of our culture and civilization are woven and that it is this fabric that gives our nation coherence and continuity. In our own time, the eminent historian and former Librarian of Congress Daniel J. Boorstin expanded on Jefferson's statement when he said, "Our democracy is based on books and reading." Without books, without writers, without publishers, without readers, without libraries and the ability to conserve and convey knowledge, our nation could hardly exist. Henry David Thoreau knew this when he stated that "books are the treasured wealth of the world and the fit inheritance of generations and nations." Without books our world could not function. We need merely consider what life was like in prehistoric times before the invention of writing and contrast that primitive and thoroughly circumscribed existence to the enormous complexity, vitality, and richness of American culture to see that, as Jefferson knew, the book is a central and defining facet of Western civilization.

Books have taken many forms through the ages. More than four thousand years ago in ancient Sumeria books were made of small blocks or tablets of clay. Without the survival of these ancient books, we would know far less about the cultures that foreshadowed our own. Their books continue to speak to us across the millennia and re-create before the mind's eye the rich textures and intellectual contours of these all but lost civilizations. In the Mediterranean world that saw the rise of the Roman Empire, the works of Homer and Virgil were written and published on sheets of a paperlike substance, papyrus, which were made into books that took the form of a long scroll or roll. But soon after the time of Christ in the first century A.D., there appeared a new form of book, the codex (a book with pages bound together). This is the form of the book we are familiar with today, almost two thousand years after it was first developed. And this fact is extraordinary. What other invention of the ancient world is still viable today? In fact, what other ancient invention has been so successful and ubiquitous that it has been seen not as ancient but as a natural and integral facet of every subsequent age? One is hard put to find an answer, and such an attempt only emphasizes the unique place the book occupies in our culture.

This form of the book is a Christian invention, but why the early Christians insisted on using a completely new format for their holy writings remains a mystery. It took several centuries for the codex book to overtake the roll, and we must assume that the final impetus for the adoption of the book across the ancient Western world was the success of Christianity.

With the collapse of the Roman Empire, Western culture was saved by the new monastic houses, primarily Benedictine, that conserved the old books and copied new ones. Had it not been for the Benedictines' reverence for books, both pagan and Christian, we would be much poorer today in literature, history, philosophy, indeed the entire culture of the ancient Western world as embodied in its books.

In the eleventh century, there was a shift away from the monasteries as centers for book production, and independent scribes began to serve the notarial and book-making needs of the growing cities. At the same time, the nascent universities created a new reading public. New texts, reference works, and commentaries were required for scholastic study, and these works were not the kind produced in monasteries. The emergence of a literate middle class in the later Middle Ages also created a demand for new types of books. These tended to be popular works of a recreational or technical nature, which were often in the vernacular.

As the fifteenth century progressed, the pressure on the book trade to produce ever larger quantities of books increased. The book trade was hard pressed to meet the demand, and the time could not have been more propitious for the introduction of a mechanical means of mass producing books. There can be little doubt that Johann Gutenberg was the inventor, not so much of the printing press, but of the manufacture of movable type, which allowed page after page of a book to be set by reusing the same stock of type over and over. Thus in a shorter period of time than it would have taken a scribe to copy a single book, a printer could reproduce a large number of exact copies of the same book. This ability to reproduce multiple copies of the same book enabled the scientific revolution that has created our modern age. It has also been argued that without the large number of printed pamphlets that fanned controversy, the Reformation, initiated by Martin Luther, would have been just another failed heresy. The ability to print with movable type has transformed our society in many ways. Francis Bacon was certainly correct when he identified printing as one of the world's three great inventions (the others being gunpowder and the compass).

Given the great demand for books in the middle of the fifteenth century, it is not surprising that the art of printing spread rapidly. By the 1470s presses were functioning in most of the countries of western Europe, and by the end of the century every major city in Europe could boast of at least one printing establishment.

When Christopher Columbus sailed from Spain, on August 3, 1492, books were undoubtedly part of the fleet's equipment and baggage. Bibles and other devotional and service books were taken as a matter of course, as were maps and navigational books. What other books may have been carried in the three small ships is a matter of conjecture. However, we can assume with some certainty that novels were also carried to the New World. The greatest bestseller of its day, *Amadís de Gaula*, was surely among the books carried across the Atlantic. We know that subsequently many copies of such novels were shipped to the Conquistadors in New Spain. These novels, emphasizing chivalric adventures in far-off lands populated by peoples blessed with fabulous riches, fired the Conquistadors' imaginations, inspiring them to strive for similar adventures and to find equally extravagant riches in the newly discovered lands. One novel in particular, Garci Rodríguez de Montalvo's *Las sergas de Esplandian*, sequel to *Amadís de Gaula*, was frequently reprinted during the years of the Conquest, and certainly played a role in shaping the Spanish vision of the Indies. This novel concerns Amazons living in California, and it is no accident that these mythological names came to be applied to geographical features in America. Hardly a ship sailed to New Spain that lacked a shipment of such novels, and their omnipresence does much to explain some aspects of the Conquest that subsequent generations have found distasteful.

The societies and cultures that were discovered in America were essentially preliterate, though books were not unheard of among the Maya and Aztecs. The Mayan peoples had developed a method of hieroglyphic notation and had crafted folded sheets of a paperlike substance made from the fibers of the maguey plant into books, which were used as divinatory almanacs by the few who were able to read, usually members of the priestly class. The Aztecs used a less sophisticated pictographic writing that was recorded on a similar paperlike substance or on animal hides and then made into books. However, in the face of superior Western technology and cultural dominance, native bookmaking technologies vanished, and many examples of native books were destroyed because of their supposed pagan contents.

With colonization, many books found their way to the New World, and most of the colonial cities were very much a part of Spain's intellectual and literary life. For example, soon after *Don Quixote* was published in the early seventeenth century, copies were circulating in Peru. Not only were books imported in large quantities from the earliest times, but in 1539 printing was introduced to the New World by the Spanish printer Juan Cromberger, who sent a press and printer, Juan Pablos, to Mexico. The first book he printed was the *Doctrina christiana en la lengua mexicana e castellana*, which seems an appropriate first title. Printing was strictly controlled by the church, and local printing was limited to missionary works, general religious titles, and textbooks. All other works were imported, including Bibles and service books. Though the importation of novels was forbidden by the church, in practice many were imported. Printing was introduced to Peru in 1584 but only spread to other colonial cities in the eighteenth century, and by the next century even reached those regions that would one day be part of the United States. In 1834 printing was introduced in California by Agustin Juan Vicente Zamorano and in New Mexico by Ramón Abreu. Ironically, in each of these cases, the presses and their equipment were imported from the United States, but the printers and their traditions came from Mexico. Even so, there was virtually no contact between the book trades of Latin America and the English-speaking peoples of the north.

I
Colonial Book Production
1638–1783

Books came to the new British colonies in North America in the baggage of the first colonists at Roanoke Island in the 1580s, Jamestown in 1607, Plymouth Colony in 1620, and the Massachusetts Bay Colony in 1629, but the capability to make books came with the first printing press, which was placed aboard the ship *John of London* bound for Massachusetts in the summer of 1638. The press was the property of the Reverend Jose Glover, formerly rector at Sutton in Surrey, who intended to put it to use in converting the Indians of New England and in publishing Puritan tracts. Though Glover was inexperienced in the art of printing, he intended to set up the press and operate it in Cambridge near the newly established Harvard College, which would also provide ample work for the press. Glover arranged for Stephen Daye and his family to accompany him on the journey. Daye was a skilled mechanic and locksmith, and Glover hoped that Daye would discover ore deposits in Massachusetts and establish an ironworks. Both Glover and Daye expected to profit greatly from this discovery of mineral wealth. Daye would certainly have re-

mained only an obscure footnote to colonial history had not the Reverend Glover died during the passage to the New World. It was left to Glover's widow to set up the press in Cambridge late in 1638, and Daye, together with his son, Matthew, undertook to operate the press.

The earliest work from the press seems to have been a small half-broadsheet entitled

The Whole Booke of Psalmes Faithfully Translated into English Metre, *commonly known as the Bay Psalm Book, was the first book printed in the American colonies, in Cambridge by Stephen Daye in 1640. The work was a new translation by Richard Mather, John Eliot, and Thomas Weld. John Cotton wrote the preface. Just over ten copies are known to survive, making this one of the world's rarest and most sought-after books.*

"The Oath of a Free-Man," an oath undertaken by the citizens of the colony in affirming their government, and *An Almanack for the Year 1639.* No copy of either item is known to survive today, and it may well be that other, similar items issued from the press at this time as well. Perhaps considering the Reverend Glover's original intentions for the press, we should be surprised at the production of these secular items. Each of these was no doubt profitable, but, more important, the first established a close working relationship with the government, and the second established the presence of the press as a commercial entity in New England. Without an owner such as the Reverend Glover or a patron such as the church or one of the missionary societies, the press could not afford to print missionary Bibles and tracts in the Indian languages, for there was no profit in it.

The first book from the press that survives to this day is the much celebrated "Bay Psalm Book" from 1640, or more correctly *The Whole Booke of Psalmes.* This modest book was edited by Richard Mather and consisted of a new metrical translation from the Hebrew. It was printed in an edition of seventeen hundred copies. This was a most fitting choice for the first substantive work to have been issued from the press. It was beyond reproach in subject matter, it was the product of one of the colony's leading men, and it was profitable. A printer could ask for nothing more, except perhaps for better equipment, supplies, and conditions. Isaiah Thomas, master printer and the first historian of American printing, said of Daye's work in 1810, "It does not exhibit the appearance of good workmanship. The compositor must have been wholly unacquainted with punctuation," and much more in the same vein.

Thomas was harsh in his judgment, though no doubt correct, but operating a press at the extreme end of the civilized world was no easy undertaking. The press, the type, the paper, and even the ink had to be imported from England. The wooden common-press had changed little since its invention in the mid-fifteenth century by Gutenberg, and the press Daye used would have been instantly familiar to the great German inventor. With the exception of the metal screw and a few other pieces, the press was wholly fashioned out of wood, which was an advantage when repairs were required. But in spite of the fact that lumber was readily available in New England, a press was not something a local carpenter could knock together. Presses were made by specialist manufacturers in England and had to be imported. The type, made from metal, had to be cast in a foundry. It was quite expensive and very heavy. In general, a printer's stock of type could last a very long time, but because the metal alloy used was relatively soft, pieces of type became worn and damaged over time. For a printer far from the foundry this was a problem without remedy, and we can surely sympathize with a colonial printer who saw the typographical quality of his work steadily decline. For the established printer, paper was the greatest single expense in producing a book, and this was doubly so for the early American printers. Like almost everything else, paper had to be imported, which naturally added to its cost. Though a printer might make his own ink, from lampblack and boiled linseed oil, there is little evidence that the earliest American printers did so. Apparently, it was easier to add ink to the long list of supplies purchased in London than to attempt local manufacture, though in time this would change.

We know almost nothing of how Daye organized his shop or conducted his business. We know he was assisted by his son, Matthew, who may have been the actual printer, but what active role the widow Glover played is unknown. In 1641 she married Henry Dunster, the first president of Harvard College, and Dunster took over management of the press, which he viewed as an official organ of the college.

Daye was not without colleagues in the book trade, at least down the river in Boston. In 1637, more than a year before

Two colonial wooden common presses of the kind used until the beginning of the nineteenth century. The press (above), old No. 1, belonged to Isaiah Thomas, the nation's first historian of printing and the founder of the American Antiquarian Society. The press occupied a special place in Thomas's life. He first learned to print on it in the 1750s, and he carried it across the Charles River on April 16, 1775, to avoid seizure by the British. Upon this press he was the first to print a report of the battles at Lexington and Concord. Though Thomas owned many presses, old No. 1 remained with him throughout his lifetime and may still be seen today at the American Antiquarian Society. Courtesy of the American Antiquarian Society. The press illustrated (below) is a replica operated by August Klapper in the Printing Office of Williamsburg, Virginia, soon after it opened in 1950. Photograph by Thomas L. Williams.

Daye began printing in Cambridge, John Sanders, a bookbinder, set up a business in Boston. We know very little about his activities as a binder, or indeed anything else, but a binder would have found ready work. The books shipped from England to be sold in the colonies typically were in sheets, unbound, and it was up to the buyer to have a newly purchased book bound as his taste and pocketbook might dictate. So it is not at all surprising that a bookbinder would appear in Massachusetts a year before the first printing press. In any case, by 1640 there were a goodly number of Bay Psalm Books in need of binding, and it may be that John Sanders was the binder who applied the sturdy calf bindings still to be seen on some of those volumes.

In the same year the Cambridge press was established, so too was the first bookstore opened. In 1638 the bookseller Hezekiah Usher arrived in Cambridge and set up shop. In 1642 he moved to Boston, sensing that the bustling port downriver was destined to be the commercial center of the colony. Usher was directly involved with the Cambridge press, as he acted at various times as agent for others in arranging printing, as publisher in his own right in contracting with the press, and as bookseller in selling and binding the products of the press. Later, when Boston became a flourishing center for the book trade, he also provided financial support to a number of printers. Usher, in fact, was a key figure in the early New England world of books and can justly be characterized as midwife to the nascent American book trade.

The Cambridge press produced a wide range of books required of the community, including a book of laws and statutes; a number of small works for Harvard College; annual almanacs; a second edition of the Bay Psalm Book; the Narragansett Declaration; a treatise on the Congregational faith; catechisms; sermons; and doctrinal treatises. It appears that Stephen Daye ended his association with the press in about 1646 and that Henry Dunster retained Matthew Daye as printer until the younger Daye's death in 1649. At that point, Henry Dunster asked Samuel Green, a former captain in the militia and doorkeeper to the Massachusetts House of Deputies with no prior experience in printing, to take over the press, and Green continued the same traditions of civic, religious, and academic printing until the press's demise in 1692. Stephen Daye tried to establish an ironworks at Nashaway, but he suffered reverses and incurred debts. He remained in Cambridge as a locksmith and sued Henry Dunster in 1656 for £100 he felt was due him for his part in establishing the press. His suit was unsuccessful, but in 1657 he successfully acquired 300 acres that had been promised him in 1641 as compensation for his efforts with the press. He died on December 22, 1668.

In 1659 Samuel Green took on an unusual apprentice. This was a young Indian, James, who subsequently took the surname of Printer. He spent about seventeen years with Green and was very useful in the printing of John Eliot's "Indian Bible" in 1663. Certainly had the Reverend Glover lived, he would have approved of this monumental undertaking of translating the Bible into the Indian language, as it had been his intention in founding the press that it should be, in part, a missionary enterprise. Instead, the press flourished by meeting the secular and spiritual needs of the colonists and not their Indian neighbors. This should

John Eliot, the apostle to the Indians, was characterized by Cotton Mather in his Magnalia Christi Americana *(1702) as one who "shone as the moon among lesser stars." Eliot's tireless work among the Indians, beginning in the 1630s, saw fruit in a series of pedagogical books and biblical translations in the language of the Massachusetts Indians that were printed at the new press in Cambridge in the 1650s and 1660s. Wood engraving from* Ballou's Pictorial Drawing-Room Companion, *April 12, 1856.*

not imply, however, that missionary tracts and pamphlets were not circulating in New England. The Corporation for Propagating the Gospel in New England, established by act of Parliament in 1649 and generally known as the New England Company, had access to presses in London that supplied its needs, and these pious tracts were readily available in New England. However, in the 1650s the company decided to undertake to print the Bible and other devotional works in the language of the local Indians and determined that it would have to be done in New England, where the translator, John Eliot, had daily access to native speakers.

A small and necessary beginning was made in 1654 when Eliot and Green printed a primer in the language of the Massachusetts Indians. The Book of Genesis and the Gospel of St. Matthew followed in 1655, and a few metrical psalms in 1658. To facilitate the larger project of printing the whole Bible, however, the company sent its agent, the Boston bookseller Hezekiah Usher, to London to obtain a new press and a quantity of appropriate equipment and type. Most important, the company arranged for an experienced printer to come from England to Green's assistance. Marmaduke Johnson knew his craft, and the quality of printing reflected his presence. It was a huge undertaking, especially for such a small and poorly equipped establishment. Even the largest of the London printing houses would have found the Indian Bible a challenging project. Green, Johnson, and their assistants labored for several years to produce fifteen hundred copies of the New Testament in 1661 (five hundred issued separately, the remaining as part of the Bible), two editions of Eliot's *Catechism* in 1662, one thousand

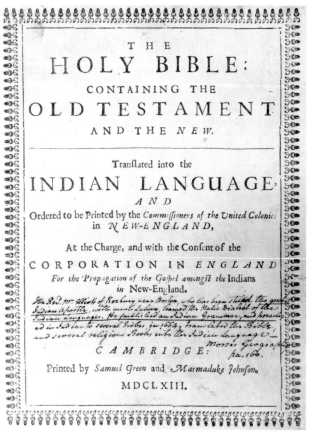

The crowning achievement of John Eliot's arduous labor of translation and of Marmaduke Johnson's equally challenging labor of printing was the Bible in the language of the Massachusetts Indians, completed in 1663. This was the first complete Bible printed in the colonies.

copies of the Bible in 1663, five hundred copies of the Psalter in 1663, and one thousand copies of Baxter's *Call to the Unconverted* in 1664, all in the Indian language.

Hezekiah Usher arranged to have the Bibles bound in Boston by a London bookbinder who had emigrated for just this purpose in 1664. John Ratcliff complained that supplies were considerably more expensive in Boston than in London and that he was able to bind only one Bible per day, thus making the whole enterprise hardly profitable. Nonetheless, Ratcliff completed the Bibles and stayed on in Boston, branching out as a bookseller and publisher as well as bookbinder.

While there can be little doubt that Marmaduke Johnson's skills as a printer ensured the success of the Indian Bible, his presence in Cambridge was highly disruptive. Printers, especially journeymen printers such as Johnson, were notorious for leading dissolute and itinerant lives. Once they had served their years of apprenticeship to a master printer, few journeymen ever found the means to rise to the status of master, either by amassing the money to buy a press or through the opportunity of marrying a master printer's widow and taking over her press. As a result, a rather large body of competent printers was in effect trapped in a life of near-poverty with little recourse for change. Johnson may have eventually seen America as a possible means to success, but at first he looked upon his three years in Massachusetts as simply a way to make money, and he had his wages remitted in England, where he had left a wife. However, in April 1662 Johnson was, as the court records indicate, indicted for "alluring the daughter of Samuel Green, printer, and drawing away her affection without the consent of her father." Johnson was convicted and fined £5; further, he was instructed to return to his wife in England. At the same time, he was fined £20 for threatening any man who might pay court to Green's daughter. In October the company was informed that the Bible was half printed but noted that Johnson had been convicted and censured in the courts, and "notwith-standing all patience and leniency used toward him he hath proved very idle and naught and absented himself from work more than half a year at one time." There is no doubt more to the story than the few facts in the surviving records illuminate, but the truth is obscure and we shall never know Johnson's side. He was allowed to stay in the colony, however, perhaps because his wife had died in England, and he and Green made peace. At this same time, perhaps because of these controversies, the government of Massachusetts appointed licensers, or censors, of the press, and in 1664 a law was passed that all printing in the colony was to be confined to Cambridge. Johnson worked with Green through 1663, but his contract was terminated the next year. In 1664 he returned to England but emigrated the following year, bringing with him a press, equipment, type, and paper, all of which allowed him to set up as a master printer. John Eliot successfully interceded with the company to make Johnson the official printer for the continuing publication of new Indian tracts. In 1665 Johnson set up his own establishment in Cambridge, where in 1670 he married, not Green's daughter but Ruth Cane. Like many a journeyman printer who managed to become a master printer, Johnson settled into a stable and solid existence. He continued to print a number of Indian-language works for John Eliot, such as the Indian grammar of 1666. He even served as constable of Cambridge in 1673. But Johnson must have felt constrained in Cambridge, for in 1674 he finally convinced the general court to allow him to move his press to Boston. This was a shrewd move on his part, as Boston was rapidly expanding into the commercial center of the colony and already boasted a small retail trade in books and bookbinding, though no printing as of yet. Soon after his move to Boston in 1675, Johnson died.

Samuel Green carried on the Cambridge press, but he was not particularly energetic. He supplemented his income as printer by selling books and supplies to the Harvard students and by cutting their hair. The press remained quite busy during the period of Eliot's Indian translations, but with the return of Marmaduke Johnson from England and the emergence of competing presses, first in Cambridge and then in Boston, the Cambridge press declined in a lassitude punctuated by an occasional job for the college, the court, and, with Johnson's death, the company. With Green's retirement in 1692, printing ceased in Cambridge and was not revived until the nineteenth century. Green's abilities as a printer had matured over the years, but perhaps his greatest contribution was in founding a dynasty of printers who spread out across the colonies and made the name Green synonymous with printing for almost two hundred years.

The opportunity that Marmaduke Johnson created in Boston was exploited by America's first native-born master printer, John Foster, who purchased Johnson's equipment and press. Boston was quite different from Cambridge, perhaps in the same way that London differed from the university cities of Cambridge and Oxford. And certainly the presses of these two colonial towns reflected those differences. The press at Cambridge was essentially a university press controlled by Harvard College. And as those who oversaw the college were the same men who controlled the church and the government, the press took on a quasi-official complexion that certainly gave it a high status but at the same time ensured that it would never reap great profits. Thus, with Green's retirement in 1692, the Cambridge press simply lapsed, having been overtaken by the far more vigorous establishments in Boston.

John Foster was unhindered by any such attachments and was able to follow a more commercial course. Foster was born in Dorchester, Massachusetts, in 1648. He attended Harvard College during the years when Green and Johnson were printing the Indian Bible, graduating in 1667. In 1669 he returned to Dorchester as a schoolmaster. During his time in Dorchester he developed a talent for engraving, and in 1674 he compiled an almanac that was printed in Cambridge in 1675. During this time Foster engraved the official seal of Massachusetts, which was first printed in a book of laws in 1672. It seems that Increase Mather, one of the press licensers, encouraged Foster to purchase Marmaduke Johnson's press, and in 1675 Foster produced the first book printed in Boston, Mather's *The Wicked Mans Portion*. Foster's press was busy and productive, producing over fifty books and broadsides between 1675 and 1681 and accounting for nearly 40 percent of New England's output. Among his most notable imprints is the first American collection of Anne Bradstreet's poetry, *Several Poems*. He printed two important accounts of King Philip's War, Increase Mather's *Brief History of the War with the Indians* in 1676, and

As Increase Mather had supported and encouraged John Foster to take over Marmaduke Johnson's defunct press in 1675, it was only fitting that the first book printed in Boston should have been Mather's The Wicked Mans Portion. *Mather was a prolific author, who wrote some 130 books and contributed to 65 other works.*

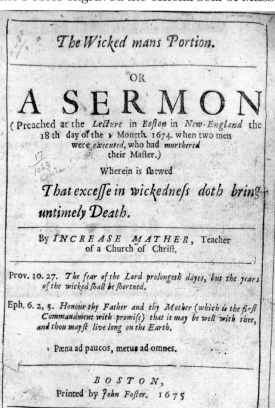

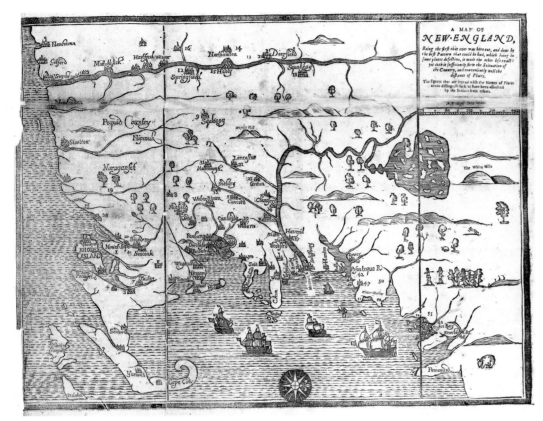

The first map engraved and printed in the colonies was Foster's engraving of New England that accompanied William Hubbard's Narrative of the Troubles with the Indians *in 1677. Courtesy of the American Antiquarian Society.*

William Hubbard's *Narrative of the Troubles with the Indians* in 1677. This later work was augmented by Foster's own engraving of a map of New England, the first to be printed in the colonies. From Foster's press also issued the first medical book to be printed in the colonies, Thomas Thacher's *Brief Rule … in the Small Pocks or Measels* in 1677. Foster continued to write and compile, print, and publish an annual almanac, always a popular item, which provided a steady income. In combining the functions of writer, printer, and publisher, Foster was quite unusual, and such a combination would not be seen again until the appearance of Benjamin Franklin in the next century. Foster seemed headed for great things, but in 1681 his life was cut short at the age of thirty-three.

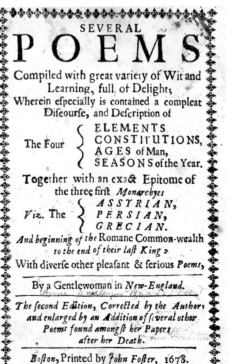

Anne Bradstreet was one of the earliest poets in the colonies. Her first book, The Tenth Muse Lately Sprung Up in America, *was published without her knowledge in 1650 in London to much acclaim on both sides of the Atlantic. The second edition, now titled* Several Poems, *was issued by John Foster in Boston in 1678 and was widely read. Cotton Mather wrote of her poems that they would stand as "a monument for her memory beyond the stateliest marbles."*

Boston was becoming a vigorous city, which developed an equally vigorous book trade by the turn of the century. Political developments made things easier for publishers and booksellers as the control of the Puritan elders weakened. There had been continual disagreements between the colonists and the English government, especially after the restoration of the English monarchy in 1660. Finally, in 1684 the colony's charter was revoked, and in 1686 the Massachusetts Bay and Plymouth Colonies were included in the Dominion of New England under Sir Edmund Andros. News of the Glorious Revolution in England prompted uprisings against Andros and the dissolution of the dominion in 1689. Two years later a royal charter was issued that incorporated Plymouth Colony and the Province of Maine within Massachusetts but placed the extended colony under a royal governor and removed the religious qualification for voting. The authority of the Puritan clergy, already much weakened, was further diminished as a result of the Salem witch trials of 1692. The clergy, notably Increase and Cotton Mather, were blamed for fanning the hysteria that led to the execution of twenty people.

With the advent of royal government, the governor took over the function of the licensers of the press, a situation that was exempt from the application of the Press Restriction Acts in force in England. And so when press restrictions and governmental censorship lapsed in England in the mid-1690s, the royal governors remained exempt and maintained their prerogatives of licensing the printing of books within their jurisdiction. In spite of the Puritan clergy's setback in the Salem witch trials, the influence of the Mathers was intensely felt by the printers of Boston, to the degree that one publisher, the Quaker Thomas Maule, was forced to go all the way to New York to find a printer who would print anything that might be considered anticlerical. In fact Maule was brought to trial in Salem in 1696 on charges of libel against government, church, and ministry in his publication of *Truth Held Forth*, which had been suppressed and burned. In spite of the fact that the judges had instructed the jury to find Maule guilty, he was pronounced not guilty. This was only the first in a series of trials that finally led to the establishment of freedom of the press as a fundamental right of the American people.

The first newspaper in the colonies, *Publick Occurrences both Forreign and Domestick* printed by R. Pierce for Benjamin Harris, appeared in Boston in 1690. It was immediately suppressed by the governor and council. The first regularly published newspaper in America was the *Boston News-Letter*. It was initially issued as a weekly on April 24, 1704, by John Campbell, postmaster of Boston, who had been writing newsletters to the New England governors. The paper was printed by Bartholomew Green, Samuel Green's son, who in 1727 became the owner and changed the name to the *Weekly News-Letter*. The paper continued until the Revolution, when it was discontinued because of its support of the British.

Massachusetts experienced accelerated growth in the early eighteenth century; settlements arose in the interior, and the Connecticut Valley was settled. Mills were built along the smaller rivers and streams to grind grain, saw logs, forge iron, and process wool. Seaport towns grew and prospered as a lucrative overseas trade flourished. The Boston book trade prospered along with the commonwealth, and, as surrounding towns and colonies also flourished, Bos-

William Bradford introduced printing into three states: Pennsylvania, New York, and New Jersey. Though a Quaker, he ran afoul of the authorities in Philadelphia soon after his arrival in 1685. Finding his freedom too restricted, he removed himself and his press to New York, where he became the crown printer in 1693. He published the first American Book of Common Prayer, the first newspaper in New York, and the first American play. In 1723 he temporarily moved a press to Perth Amboy in New Jersey, where he printed a volume for the state assembly, establishing yet another milestone, the first book printed in New Jersey. Drawing by A. L. Schropter.

ton printers and booksellers moved into new markets and brought the art of printing to new towns. Printing came to Connecticut in 1708, to Rhode Island in 1727, to New Hampshire in 1756, and to Vermont in 1778 or 1779.

Printing first came to Pennsylvania when William Bradford emigrated to Philadelphia in 1685. Born in 1663, Bradford had grown up in the London book trade and had been apprenticed to the successful Quaker master printer Andrew Soule, who not only taught him the trade but also introduced him to the Society of Friends. In 1685 he married Soule's daughter, Elizabeth, and the newlyweds immediately embarked for Pennsylvania. The first item issued from Bradford's newly established shop in Philadelphia was an almanac, usually a safe and profitable venture. His "Printer to the Readers" statement in the almanac illustrates his outlook and the difficulties he faced as a pioneer printer:

> Hereby understand that after great Charge and Trouble, I have brought that great Art and Mystery of Printing to this part of America believing it may be of great service to you in several respects, hoping to find Encouragements, not only in this Almanack, but what else I shall enter upon for the use and service of the Inhabitants of these Parts. Some Irregularities,

there be in this Diary, which I desire you to pass by this year; for being lately come hither, my Matereals were Misplaced, and out of order, whereupon I was forced to use Figures & Letters of various sizes, but understanding the want of something of this nature, and being importuned thereto, I ventured to make publick this, desiring you to accept thereof, and by the next, (as I find encouragement) shall endeavour to have things compleat. And for the ease of Clarks, Scrivniers, &c. I propose to print blank Bills, Bonds, Letters of Attourney, Indentures, Warrants, &c. and what else presents itself, wherein I shall be ready to serve you; and remain your Friend W. Bradford.

Whatever encouragement Bradford may have found from his readers, he found little immediate encouragement from the authorities. He was called before the provincial council and ordered to remove the courtesy title "Lord," which appeared in a list of historical dates and events: "The beginning of the government here by Lord Penn."

Four years later Bradford again ran afoul of the authorities when he printed the charter of the colony. He was called before the council, where he made an eloquent plea for the freedom of the press: "If I may not print such things as come to my hand … I cannot live. If I print one thing to-day, and the contrary party bring me another to-morrow, to contradict it, I cannot say that I shall not print it. Printing is a manufacture of the nation, and therefore ought rather to be encouraged than suppressed." But the council viewed the press as a potential threat to government, which required close control.

Bradford was an energetic man who, together with Samuel Carpenter and William Rittenhouse, established a papermill in Germantown in 1691. This was the first papermill in the colonies, and it flourished for many years, providing colonial printers with much cheaper paper than could be imported from England. This marked the first major step in creating an independent book trade in the colonies.

The council once again exercised its control over the press in 1692 when Bradford printed a tract for a dissenting faction within the Society of Friends. He was arrested and his press and equipment confiscated, including the offending pamphlet still set in type. At the trial no witness could be produced to testify that Bradford had actually printed the tract, but the prosecution had the confiscated standing type, which was passed among the jury until one clumsy juror dropped it and it fell to pieces, as did the prosecution's case. Even so, Bradford had come to the end of his patience with attempts at press censorship in the City of Brotherly Love, and in 1693 he became crown printer in New York, where he remained for fifty years. From the safety of New York, he printed a scathing account of press censorship in Pennsylvania,

New-England's Spirit of Persecution Transmitted to Pennsilvania. In his first year in New York he printed between thirty and forty items, mostly acts, proclamations, and the like. He printed the first record of American legislative proceedings in 1695, New York's first paper currency in 1709, and its first newspaper in 1725, the *New York Gazette.*

In 1725 Bradford took on as partner his former apprentice, John Peter Zenger, who in the following year opened his own printing establishment. In 1730 Zenger printed the first arithmetic textbook published in the colonies. Three years

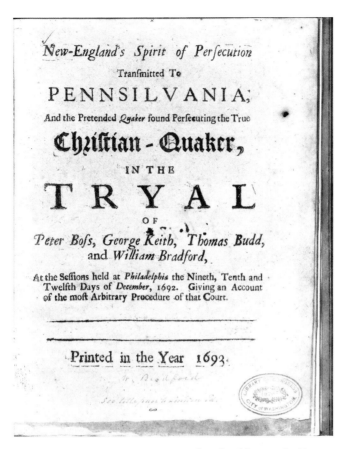

Soon after William Bradford quit Philadelphia and settled in New York he published an account of the intolerance he had endured in the City of Brotherly Love in George Keith's New-England's Spirit of Persecution Transmitted to Pennsilvania.

later, he founded the *New York Weekly Journal,* a newspaper backed by an influential group to oppose the government-controlled *New York Gazette* published by Bradford. Zenger printed his backers' articles criticizing the governor of New York, and on November 17, 1734, he was arrested and imprisoned on charges of seditious libel. During the trial, which took place in 1735, after he had spent nine months in prison, Zenger's lawyer eloquently argued that the allegations printed in the *Journal* were true and therefore not libelous. Despite the contrary opinion of the judge, the jury declared Zenger not guilty. This verdict was a major milestone in the history of American freedom of the press. Zenger was appointed public printer for the colony of New York in 1737 and that of New Jersey in 1738. He continued to publish the *Weekly Journal* until his death in 1746.

Bradford also introduced printing to New Jersey. In 1723 he went to Perth Amboy to print an issue of paper money for New Jersey and at the same time printed a volume of the New Jersey Assembly's acts. In 1728 Samuel Keimer and Benjamin Franklin went to Burlington, New Jersey, for the same purpose and also printed a volume of acts. However, the first permanent press was established in 1754 in Woodbridge by James Parker, who became government printer in 1758.

James Rivington was one of the most colorful and controversial printers and publishers in colonial America. Arriving in New York in 1760, he set out to create a chain of bookstores but soon turned to other endeavors, including a lottery, which ruined him. Never down for long, he began publishing a newspaper in 1773 with a distinct Tory bias. In 1775 the Sons of Liberty broke into his shop and destroyed his presses and all his equipment. He was forced to retreat to London but was soon back in New York with the British occupation. Rivington taunted the American patriots in his newspaper during the war years and by the end of the war was one of the most hated Tories in New York. To everyone's astonishment, it was revealed that he had actually been a spy for George Washington. By playing both sides, the cagey bookseller and publisher just barely managed to avoid disaster. Engraving by A. H. Ritchie.

Andrew Bradford, a son of William Bradford born in Philadelphia in 1686, learned the trade in his father's New York establishment. In 1712 he founded his own press in Philadelphia and, in 1719, Pennsylvania's first newspaper, the *American Weekly Mercury*, which rivaled Benjamin Franklin's *Gazette*. His short-lived *American Magazine* (1741) is considered the first colonial magazine. Andrew's nephew, William Bradford, was born in New York City in 1721. He also entered the book trade and ran a bookstore, a coffee house, an insurance company, and one of the most successful presses of the time. His *Pennsylvania Journal, or Weekly Advertiser* (founded in 1742), criticized the 1765 Stamp Act and urged unification of the colonies. William's son, Thomas Bradford, who was born in Philadelphia in 1745, edited the *Pennsylvania Journal* with his father until 1778, when he assumed full control. He founded the *Merchants' Daily Advertiser* in 1797, an early financial bulletin. In 1798 its name was changed to the *True American*, and it introduced the nation's first literary supplement.

New York's most colorful printer, publisher, and bookseller during this period was James Rivington. Rivington's father, Charles, was an eminent publisher in London, and when he died in 1742, James and his brother John continued the business until 1756, when James set up his own business. He had an excellent business sense, and the firm prospered. However, as the firm reaped profits, Rivington indulged his taste for gambling, women, and expensive living. Surviving bankruptcy, he decided to emigrate to New York. He arrived in 1760, establishing bookshops in Philadelphia and New York, and one in Boston in 1762. He intended to establish a whole chain of bookshops, but by 1765 he changed his mind and concentrated on his New York establishment. Soon after, in 1766, he sponsored a highly questionable enterprise in Annapolis; this was the Maryland Lottery, which involved land sales and bankrupted him for a second time. Not long after, however, he was back in business in New York and in 1767 published his first book in America. Rivington settled down and became one of the city's more responsible and substantial citizens. In 1773 he began publishing a newspaper with the extraordinary title of *Rivington's New York Gazetteer; or the Connecticut, New Jersey, Hudson's River, and Quebec Weekly Advertiser.*

Rivington used the paper to promote his Tory political beliefs, and soon the paper was the premier Tory paper in America. Naturally, Rivington was considered a foe by the Sons of Liberty, and as the political situation heated up, his position became more and more tenuous. He was arrested in early 1775, and under duress signed an affidavit supporting the patriots. However, it soon became apparent to the Sons of Liberty that he remained an ardent Tory, and on November 27, 1775, they broke into his shop and destroyed his presses and all his equipment. He had no choice but to take ship to London and wait for the crisis to pass.

As the war seemed to go against the Americans and the British occupied New York, Rivington returned in triumph on September 24, 1777. He resumed publication of the *Gazetteer* and used it to great effect to ridicule and insult the American cause and leaders, in particular George Washington and Ethan Allen. In fact, he so ridiculed Allen that the general vowed that he would "lick Rivington the very first opportunity." As the war ended, Rivington was prohibited from conducting business. However, when it was learned that he had been a spy for Washington (Rivington had successfully played both sides of the street, but few believed he had really been a secret patriot), he was allowed to apologize for his conduct in publishing the *Gazetteer* during the war and resume his bookselling, though not his publishing, business. Soon after, General Ethan Allen came looking for him, and the episode is best retold in Rivington's own words:

I was sitting after a good dinner, alone, with my bottle of Madeira before me, when I heard an unusual noise in the street, and a huzza from the boys. I was in the second story, and stepping to the window, saw a tall figure in tarnished regimentals, with a large cocked hat and an enormous long sword, followed by a crowd of boys, who occasionally cheered him with huzzas, of which he seemed insensible. He came up to my door and stopped. I could see no more. My heart told me it was Ethan Allen. I shut down my window and retired behind my table and bottle. I was certain the hour of reckoning had come. There was no retreat.

Mr. Staples, my clerk, came in paler than ever, and clasping his hands, said, "Master, he is come. ... He entered the store, and asked if James Rivington lived there. I answered, 'Yes, sir,' 'Is he at home?' 'I will go and see, sir,' I said; and now, master, what is to be done? There he is in the store, and the boys peeping at him from the street."

I had made up my mind. I looked at the bottle of Madeira—possibly took a glass. "Show him up," said I; "and if such Madeira can not mollify him, he must be harder than adamant."

There was a fearful moment of suspense. I heard him on the stairs, his long sword clanking at every step. In he stalked.

"Is your name James Rivington?"

"It is, sir, and no man could be more happy than I am to see [General] Ethan Allen."

"Sir, I have come—"

"Not another word, my dear [General], until you have taken a seat and a glass of old Madeira."

"But, sir, I don't think it proper—"

"Not another word, [General]. Taste this wine; I have had it in glass for ten years. Old wine, you know, unless it is originally sound, never improves by age."

He took the glass, swallowed the wine, smacked his lips, and shook his head approvingly.

"Sir, I have come—"

"Not another word until you have taken another glass, and then, my dear [General], we will talk of old affairs, and I have some droll events to detail."

In short, we finished two bottles of Madeira, and parted as good friends as if we never had cause to be otherwise.

Benjamin Franklin was eighteenth-century America's foremost man of letters, with a worldwide reputation. He began life as a printer and publisher and never left that persona behind, preferring to style himself simply as "the Printer of Philadelphia." He was a great collector of books and founded the Library Company of Philadelphia. At the end of his life he donated 4,276 books to the Library Company, the American Philosophical Society, Yale, and Harvard. His autobiography has become a national classic that has shaped the values and perspectives of generations. From a Pictorial Life of Benjamin Franklin *by John Frost, 1846.*

Rivington prospered in bookselling for a time, but in 1797 he was jailed for bad debts, and soon after his release he died, in 1802, on the Fourth of July.

There can be no greater contrast to the epicurean and sensuous Tory Rivington, than Benjamin Franklin, one of the most remarkable men of his extraordinary generation. For all his substantial accomplishments as businessman, scientist and inventor, author and moralist, community organizer, and politician and diplomat, he continued to style himself simply as the "Printer of Philadelphia," an appellation that gave him great satisfaction throughout his long and full life. Franklin was born in Boston on January 17, 1706, the tenth son and seventeenth child of Josiah Franklin, a tallow chandler and soap boiler. After less than two years of formal schooling, he was pressed into his father's trade making soap and candles. At the age of twelve he was apprenticed to his brother James, printer of the *New England Courant*, where he read virtually every book that came through the shop. At the age of sixteen, he wrote some pieces for the *Courant* signed Silence Dogood, in which he satirized the Boston authorities

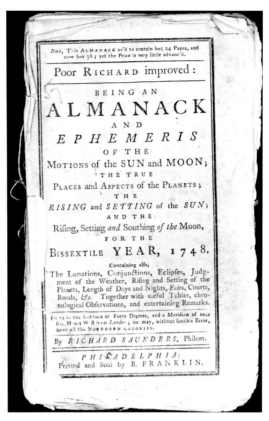

Poor Richard's Almanack *was written and published by Benjamin Franklin from 1733 to 1758. Certainly the most famous of American almanacs, Poor Richard's was well known throughout the colonies and exerted an immense influence in shaping the American character. Franklin's characters, Richard and Bridget Saunders, conveyed Franklin's humor and homely wisdom to many readers, and in time these characters became associated with the frugality and virtue that many believed distinguished Americans from other nationalities.*

and society. At one point James Franklin was imprisoned for printing such pieces, and the paper was carried on in Benjamin's name.

In 1723 Benjamin ran away to New York and then Philadelphia. Though nearly penniless and unknown, he soon made friends and found a job as a printer. After a year he went to England, where he worked diligently and became extraordinarily proficient as a printer. Returning to Philadelphia in 1726, he soon owned his own newspaper, the *Pennsylvania Gazette*, and in 1732 he began to print *Poor Richard's Almanack*. His business prospered and expanded further when he contracted to do the public printing of the province and established partnerships with printers in other colonies. He also operated a bookshop and became clerk of the Pennsylvania Assembly and postmaster of Philadelphia.

One of his most notable accomplishments was the establishment of the nation's first public library in 1731, which he recounts in his *Autobiography:*

> And now I set on foot my first project of a public nature, that for a subscription library. I drew up the proposals … and … procured fifty subscribers. … We afterwards obtain'd a charter, the company being increased to one hundred: this was the mother of all the North American subscription

libraries, now so numerous. It is become a great thing itself, and continually increasing. These libraries have improved the general conversation of the Americans, made the common tradesmen and farmers as intelligent as most gentlemen from other countries, and perhaps have contributed in some degree to the stand so generally made throughout the colonies in defense of their privileges.

The library created by Franklin and his friends, the Library Company of Philadelphia, is today one of the nation's most significant research libraries.

By 1748, Franklin was personally able to withdraw from the printing business and effectively retire on the income generated by the business. This enabled him to turn his attention to other subjects and endeavors.

Franklin's early years in the book trade are very well described in his *Autobiography,* and his tale of honesty, diligence, and perseverance, having become a standard school text, has formed part of the nation's character. His firsthand account of the trade in the 1720s and 1730s provides us with an unparalleled view of the colonial printer's lot. Upon his arrival in Philadelphia in 1723 he found two printing houses.

[Samuel] Keimer's printing-house, I found, consisted of an old shatter'd press, and one small, worn-out font of English. … I endeavor'd to put his press (which he had not yet us'd, and of which he understood nothing) into order fit to be work'd with; and, promising to come and print off his Elegy as soon as he should have got it ready, I return'd to [Andrew] Bradford's. … These two printers I found poorly qualified for their business. Bradford had not been bred to it, and was very illiterate; and Keimer, tho' something of a scholar, was a mere compositor, knowing nothing of presswork.

Bradford had the wealth of his family behind him, but Keimer was destined to fail, as Franklin immediately perceived. As we view Keimer through Franklin's eyes, we share his disdain and disgust for his mismanagement and for wasted opportunities, but in fact Keimer was not untypical of many colonial printers. He suffered from his own ignorance and arrogance, poorly trained apprentices, and worn equipment and type. Upon Franklin's return from London in 1796, he once again worked for Keimer.

Our printing-house often wanted sorts, and there was no letter-founder in America; I had seen types cast at James's in London, but without much attention to the manner; however, I now contrived a mould, made use of the letters we had as puncheons, struck the matrices in lead, and thus supply'd in a pretty tolerable way all deficiencies. I also engrav'd several things on occasion; I made the ink; I was warehouseman, and everything, and, in short, quite a factotum.

Franklin's diligence and skills revived Keimer's business for a time, but as Keimer's apprentices learned the trade from Franklin, Keimer felt he could dispense with Franklin, and they parted company. Franklin set up his own shop and worked diligently to make it a success.

One night, when, having impos'd my forms, I thought my day's work over, one of them by accident was broken, and two pages reduced to pi, I immediately distributed and compos'd it over again before I went to bed; and this industry, visible to our neighbors, began to give us character and credit; particularly, I was told, that mention being made of the new printing-office at the merchants' Every-night club, the general opinion was that it must fail, there being already two printers in the place, Keimer and Bradford; but Dr. Baird … gave a contrary opinion: "For the industry of that Franklin," says he, "is superior to any thing I ever saw of the kind; I see him still at work when I go home from club, and he is at work again before his neighbors are out of bed."

Franklin's subsequent success was well justified and much of the credit for raising the standards of book production in the colonies must go to him. In addition, the center of the book trade shifted south to Philadelphia, due in great part to his growing success and stature.

Virginia's first printer, William Nuthead, arrived in Jamestown in 1682 and commenced printing the acts of the recently adjourned Virginia Assembly, always a potentially troublesome body for the Crown. When the governor and members of the Crown Council realized what Nuthead was doing, he was called before the council and ordered to cease all printing until a judgment could be obtained from London. After the passage of several months, a new governor, Lord Francis Howard of Effingham, landed with royal orders that "no person be permitted to use any press for printing upon any occasion whatsoever." There could be no doubt as to the meaning of this explicit mandate, and thus Nuthead was forced to leave Virginia. The ban on printing was quite effective and was maintained for nearly fifty years, until William Parks established a press in Williamsburg in 1730.

In 1732 Parks was appointed public printer for the colony, a position that insured his standing in Virginia and the profitability of his press. Parks had extensive experience in both England and Maryland before coming to Virginia, and, in addition to being a competent master printer, he was also a man of letters. Thus his output was not only well printed but also included literary items not often found in a colonial printer's output. One of the more interesting of these items is John Markland's *Typographia, an Ode on Printing*, the first American contribution to the literature on printing. In 1736 Parks established the *Virginia Gazette*, which he continued to issue until his death in 1750.

When William Nuthead was forced to cease printing in Virginia in 1684, he moved to St. Mary's City, the capital of Maryland, and set up his press in mid-1685. He printed mostly for the assembly until his death in 1695 at the age of forty-one. His widow, Dinah, took over the press and moved it to the new capital, Annapolis. Dinah Nuthead was the first in a long line of American women who made significant contributions in the trade, and this achievement is even more remarkable as she was illiterate, unable even to sign her name. She managed to master the alphabet and thus set type but could not read what she was setting. Very little, beyond a few printed forms, survives from Dinah Nuthead's press. Maryland's first newspaper, the *Maryland Gazette*, was established by William Parks (who subsequently returned printing to Virginia) in 1727 in Annapolis.

In May 1731, the government of South Carolina offered the equivalent of £175 sterling to the first printer who would set up shop in Charleston. Soon there were three printers vying for the prize, two of whom were serious contestants. One of these, Eleazer Phillips of Boston, had been solicited by the Commons House of Assembly, composed of the leading colonists, and the other, Thomas Whitemarsh of Philadelphia, had come on his own initiative. The governor and Crown Council began to favor Whitemarsh and challenged the assembly to a contest between the two printers. Each printer was to be given an identical piece of copy for printing, "and then," said the members of the council, "we shall judge who can the best serve the Publick." Unfortunately, the assembly would have none of it. As the assembly's candidate, Phillips received the prize, but Whitemarsh petitioned for redress and was awarded the equivalent of £35. Phillips established the *South Carolina Weekly Journal* in January 1732, but he died in July. Whitemarsh succeeded him and founded the *South Carolina Gazette*, but he too soon died, in September 1733. Benjamin Franklin continued the story in his *Autobiography:*

> In 1733 I sent one of my journeymen [Lewis Timothy] to Charleston, South
> Carolina, where a printer was wanting. I furnish'd him with a press and let-
> ters, on an agreement of partnership, by which I was to receive one-third of

the profits of the business, paying one-third of the expense. He was a man of learning, and honest but ignorant in matters of account; and, tho' he sometimes made me remittances, I could get no account from him, nor any satisfactory state of our partnership while he lived. On his decease, the business was continued by his widow, who … not only sent me as clear a state as she could find of the transactions past, but continued to account with the greatest regularity and exactness every quarter afterwards, and managed the business with such success, that she not only brought up reputably a family of children, but, at the expiration of the term, was able to purchase of me the printing-house, and establish her son in it.

And so finally printing was firmly established in South Carolina. Elizabeth Timothy died in 1757, by which time the business had been carried on in the name of her son, Peter, for seventeen years.

The last of the colonies to acquire a printer was Georgia. And this is somewhat surprising given the history and circumstances of its founding. In 1732, James Oglethorpe and nineteen associates secured a charter to colonize Georgia, and in 1733 they founded Savannah. Oglethorpe envisioned Georgia as a refuge for both Protestant dissenters and those who had served time in debtor's prison. He intended to provide a new life in the New World and to reform the idle and criminal classes of England. Given his enlightened outlook, it is odd that the manufacture of books and the establishment of a newspaper did not figure high on his list of requirements for the new colony. In any case, long after Oglethorpe had quit the colony in failure in 1743 and relinquished the colony's charter to the crown in 1752, a printer, James Johnson, arrived from England, in 1762. Johnson soon secured the position of printer to the government and on April 7, 1763, established the *Georgia Gazette*, which continued until 1776. The newspaper was resumed in 1783 and only ceased publication in 1802, when Johnson announced that because of his age and poor health he was unable to carry on.

John Adams noted that "a native American who cannot read and write is as rare as a comet or earthquake." Though Adams may have exaggerated somewhat, it was true that the American

John Adams, the nation's first vice president and second president, was an avid book collector and author. He owned the works of all the major classical authors. For Adams reading was a political act and the duty of a citizen, so that, he said, "my sons may have liberty to study mathematics and philosophy … in order to give their children a right to study painting, poetry, music." From the Boston Magazine, *1784.*

colonists were one of the most literate peoples in the world. Most
colonists could read, although we
cannot be sure how proficient
many people were and there was
certainly a literacy gap between
men and women. Nonetheless,
books and other printed matter
were very much a part of almost
every household. At the very
least, even the most humble
household contained a Bible and
an almanac. Newspapers were
also very much in evidence, but
they were not cherished and
saved from generation to generation as books were. Because the
American colonies were an appendage of the mother country, almost everything of
a manufactured nature came from Britain. This was certainly true for the book trade,
but with certain significant exceptions. It was always cheaper and easier to produce
a large edition in London and ship part of it to the colonies, rather than print the
edition in one of the colonial cities. Thus an educated American desiring to purchase books of literature, history, religion, and the like might well make his purchase from a colonial bookseller, but the books would have come from London.
Textbooks and schoolbooks and works of a technical or scientific nature also came
from London. Most American printers were sustained by newspapers, and the few
books that they printed were generally of local interest, such as political and religious tracts, narratives of Indian wars, public executions, and local histories, abridged
or cheaper editions of standard works, and almanacs.

The distribution of books was a daunting task. Geography and lack of transportation created huge obstacles that were never completely overcome. The nascent
distribution system consisted of informal networks of friends, itinerant peddlers,
temporary laborers hired by printers to hawk newly published books and ballads in
towns, bookstore owners (who usually sold many other things beside books), independent agents, and institutional libraries and individuals who imported books from
abroad. The quickest method for distributing a book may have been to reprint it.
When Thomas Paine's *Common Sense* was published in Philadelphia in 1776 by Robert

Bell, the printer found himself unable to supply the demand beyond Philadelphia quickly enough. Many printers in other towns and cities, even as close as Lancaster, Pennsylvania, printed their own copies for distribution in their own areas. Had an efficient system of transportation existed, Bell might have supplied all of the colonies, but the distribution system, such as it was, was strictly local.

Since the introduction of the first printing press to Massachusetts, the almanac had been the quintessential product of the colonial printer. Almost every printer produced one, as it was almost guaranteed to turn a good profit. But the almanac was more than just a profitable book; issued annually, it came to epitomize the American condition and conversely to shape a distinctly American view-

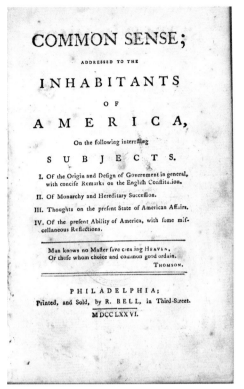

Thomas Paine's Common Sense *took the colonies by storm. It was first published on January 10, 1776, in Philadelphia and was quickly reprinted up and down the colonies. By June 1776 it had sold 120,000 copies, a phenomenal number for a time when a sale of over 20,000 constituted a bestseller. Paine's arguments for an immediate declaration of independence carried the day and propelled the colonies on a revolutionary course.* Common Sense *would go on to sell half a million copies in Paine's lifetime.*

point. People relied on almanacs for all kinds of information, such as distances between towns, the times of sunrise and sunset, the schedules of tides, the names of tavern keepers, weather predictions, the sessions of courts, important events and dates, recipes, lists of public officials, and occasional poems and stories. Franklin's *Poor Richard's Almanack* is the best known of the colonial almanacs and was distinguished by its sayings and maxims. Franklin described it best in his *Autobiography:*

> In 1732 I first publish'd my Almanack, under the name of Richard Saunders; it was continu'd by me about twenty-five years, commonly call'd Poor Richard's Almanack. I endeavor'd to make it both entertaining and useful, and it accordingly came to be in such demand, that I reap'd considerable profit from it, vending annually near ten thousand. And observing that it was generally read, scarce any neighborhood in the province being without it, I consider'd it as a proper vehicle for conveying instruction among the common people, who bought scarcely any other books; I therefore filled all the little spaces that occurr'd between the remarkable days in the calendar with proverbial sentences, chiefly such as inculcated industry and frugality, as the means of procuring wealth, and thereby securing virtue; it being more difficult for a man in want, to act always honestly, as, to use

here one of those proverbs, it is hard for an empty sack to stand upright. These proverbs, which contained the wisdom of many ages and nations, I assembled and form'd into a connected discourse prefix'd to the Almanack of 1757, as the harangue of a wise old man to the people attending an auction. The bringing all these scatter'd counsels thus into a focus enabled them to make greater impression. The piece, being universally approved, was copied in all the newspapers of the Continent; reprinted in Britain on a broad side, to be stuck up in houses; two translations were made of it in French, and great numbers bought by the clergy and gentry, to distribute gratis among their poor parishioners and tenants. In Pennsylvania, as it discouraged useless expense in foreign superfluities, some thought it had its share of influence in producing that growing plenty of money which was observable for several years after its publication.

In the years leading up to the Revolution, almanacs became vehicles for spreading political doctrine and revolutionary views, and their influence on the common reader was every bit as significant as the influence of newspapers on the more educated reader. In early 1766, the leading producer of almanacs, Nathaniel Ames, used

Thomas Jefferson was a lifelong book collector. But unlike some collectors, Jefferson read his books and created his library to serve as an intellectual repository from which he could draw strength and wisdom as he came to grips with the great issues of the day. There can be no doubt that the author of the Declaration of Independence was well served in his choice of books. Engraving by T. Johnson, based on the painting by Gilbert Stuart in Century Magazine, *May 1887.*

his almanacs to attack the Stamp Act and asserted that God would defend America from "those who would oppress or tyrannize over us." Some almanacs went so far as to instruct readers in making and storing gunpowder. Of course, the almanac was not limited to America and was to be found across the Western world in many forms, but given the broad—if sometimes shallow—literacy of the American population, the American almanac played a unique role in bringing information to even the most humble household.

If almanacs were shaping popular opinion, so too were more traditional books shaping the perspectives of the Founding Fathers. Thomas Jefferson, a lifelong collector of books, selected many of his volumes for specific purposes. He was especially interested in history that might shed light on the question of government and individual rights. His selection of books—almost all acquired from England or the Continent—enabled him to do extensive reading that shaped his attitude about the nature of individual rights, influencing his actions throughout his life and in turn influencing the form of government adopted by the United States.

Written primarily by Madison, the Virginia Plan (May 29, 1787) presented his vision of a federal constitution to the Convention. It was opposed by the smaller states, which wanted equal representation.

Jefferson's ideas and philosophy also shaped the creation and growth of the nation's premier cultural institution, the Library of Congress, which in turn has provided national leadership that has exerted a profound influence on the growth and direction of libraries of all kinds—public, school, academic, state, federal, corporate, and others—that endures to this day. Jefferson believed the Library, which was founded in 1800, should be universal and its collections comprehensive. He pointed out that there was "no subject to which a member of Congress may not have occasion to refer." And indeed it is this philosophy of universality and access, extended to the nation as a whole, that has created a true national library. Jefferson's contributions did not end when he left office in 1809. After the British had burned the Capitol and the Library in 1814, he offered to sell his personal library of 6,487 volumes to Congress to replace the destroyed collection. Congress agreed in 1815, and Jefferson's wide-ranging and comprehensive collection became the foundation on which one of the world's greatest libraries has been built.

Jefferson was instrumental in opening up the world of books to his fellow Founding Fathers with equally profound results. The large quantities of books that

Jefferson's library was almost literally an extension of his mind. When he offered to part with his 6,487-volume collection (the finest private library in America at that time) to replace the books of the Library of Congress destroyed by British troops in 1814, it was an act of great magnanimity and patriotism. For Jefferson, a man who admitted he could not live without books, it was a supreme sacrifice. Having sold his library, he immediately began collecting new books. Jefferson's library is the core of the Library of Congress, and as an extension of his mind and a reflection of his outlook, it has established Jefferson's vision of comprehensiveness and universality for the Library of Congress that endures to this day. Photograph by Reid Baker.

James Madison greatly profited from Jefferson's careful selection of books for him during Jefferson's sojourn in Europe in 1784. From Madison's intense and careful historical research came his vision for a constitution. Statue of Madison in the Great Hall of the James Madison Building of the Library of Congress. Photograph by Jim Higgins.

America's oldest national cultural institution and the largest library in the world, the Library of Congress contains over 110 million items on more than 530 miles of shelf space, including films, maps, prints, drawings, videos, CD-ROMs, newspapers, manuscripts, journals, and books in more than 450 languages. Each day the collections increase by seven thousand items. Established as a legislative library in 1800, it continues to serve that important and essential function, but during the last two centuries its mission has expanded to encompass the role of a national library, providing national and international leadership for libraries and information agencies. This transformation accelerated in 1870 when the Library began to receive one copy of every book, pamphlet, map, or other printed material registered for copyright. The Library was better able to serve the public after 1897, upon completion of the Jefferson Building, which included public reading rooms and exhibition space for the first time. In 1902 Congress authorized the Library to make its cataloguing records available to libraries across the country, thereby providing a vital service to the nation that continues to this day. In 1914 Congress created the Legislative Reference Service (now the Congressional Research Service) to provide specialized services for the Library's original constituents. In recognition of the Library's role as a national library, Congress has authorized the establishment of the National Library Service for the Blind and Physically Handicapped (1931), the American Folklife Center (1976), the American Television and Radio Archives (1976), the Center for the Book (1977), and the National Film Preservation Board (1988), all within the Library of Congress. With the approach of the twenty-first century, the Library is taking a leadership role in creating and implementing a National Digital Library, whose mission is to digitize and make available five million manuscripts, photographs, films, musical scores, and other materials representing the core of American creativity by early in the new millennium. Photograph by Jim Higgins.

First page of Madison's notes from the Constitutional Convention. Madison's vision and strength of will was largely responsible for the Convention being held. For nearly four months, beginning in May 1787, fifty-five delegates from twelve states debated and considered what the future organization and structure of the United States should be.

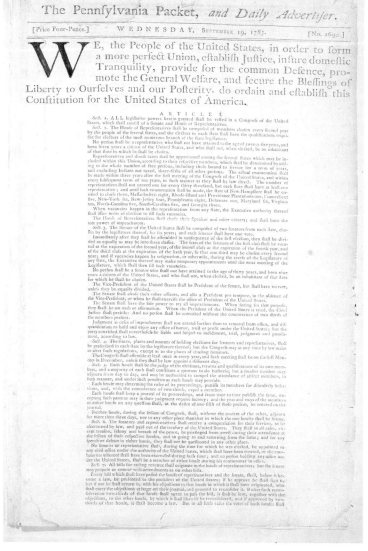

After nearly four months of intense debate and negotiation a compromise constitution was agreed upon on September 17 and printed two days later in the Pennsylvania Packet and Daily Advertiser *on September 19, 1787.*

he purchased in France for James Madison had a significant impact on Madison's approach to constitutional issues. In the winter of 1785–86 Madison delved into a historical study of ancient and modern confederacies. From this intensive analysis came his "Vices of the Political System of the United States," which was available to the delegates just before they convened in Philadelphia in 1787 to consider a new form of government. Though Madison's vision of what form the Constitution should take was not fully realized, no one can doubt that the Constitution would have been quite different without his vision.

Similarly for John Adams, writing in 1780, reading was a political act:

I must study politics and war, that my sons may have liberty to study mathematics and philosophy, geography, natural history and naval architecture, navigation, commerce, and agriculture, in order to give their children a right to study painting, poetry, music, architecture, statuary, tapestry, and porcelain.

Jefferson, Madison, Adams, and almost all the other Founding Fathers read extensively and were very much a part of the intellectual world that was conveyed to them in large measure through books. Jefferson's statement, "I cannot live without books," could well be the collective *cri de coeur* of the Founding Fathers and indeed of the nation itself.

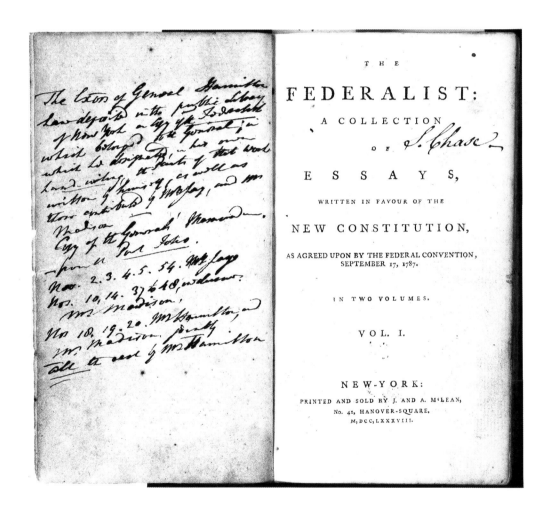

In spite of the great compromise achieved in the Constitution, many people across the country were not at all convinced that it should be accepted. In an effort to build support for the new Constitution, Alexander Hamilton, James Madison, and John Jay wrote eighty-five essays signed with the pseudonym Publius. They originally appeared as letters in various newspapers, in which the new Constitution was explained and acceptance advocated. The first thirty-six essays were published in March 1788 and the final forty-nine in May 1789. A collection of all eighty-five essays, The Federalist, *has come to be especially valued as an explication of the principles behind the Constitution and James Madison's own copy even more so for its extensive annotations.*

II
Publishing in the New Nation
1784–1820

With the success of the Revolution and the establishment of the United States, the American book trade began to cut many of its ties with the mother country and in time became a self-sufficient industry. This is especially true in the creation of viable papermaking and typefounding industries, as well as in the increasing tariff placed on books imported from Britain. The contrast between the pre-Revolutionary colonial printer and the post-Revolutionary publisher is striking, and this transformation is best exemplified in the career of Isaiah Thomas, who began as a colonial printer and ended as one of the greatest book publishers in the United States.

Isaiah Thomas was born in Boston on January 19, 1749. His father, Moses Thomas, had tried a series of careers—tailor, sailor, soldier, storekeeper, schoolmaster, and farmer—and had little success. He married Fidelity Grant of Rhode Island, who bore him five children before he died, nearly penniless, in 1752. The Thomas children were sent out to relatives and friends, and when Isaiah, the youngest, was six, he was apprenticed to the printer Zechariah Fowle. His indenture was to run until he was twenty-one years of age. Fowle looked upon young Isaiah as more of a servant than an apprentice, and he was set to work as a domestic. Only after the passage of some time was he allowed to begin his study of the art of printing. Fowle was a poor teacher and, as Thomas later commented, "an indifferent hand at presswork and much worse at the case." Nonetheless, the young Isaiah had found his calling and required remarkably little instruction. He must have been quite a sight as he walked along a bench that enabled him to reach the cases. Soon he had composed his first piece, a bawdy ballad, "The Lawyer's Pedigree." This feat was all the more remarkable in that the boy, though familiar with the alphabet, could not read. Fowle was obliged under the contract of indenture to provide the boy with an education, but Isaiah was forced to educate himself using Fowle's Bible and dictionary. Fowle took on a partner, Samuel Draper, in 1758, and during the three years of the partnership, Isaiah learned a

Isaiah Thomas was the leading publisher in the decades following the Revolutionary War. His printing, publishing, and bookselling business was centered in Worcester but included a major publishing enterprise in Boston under the name of Thomas and Andrews and many retail bookstores across New England and the Middle Atlantic states. Portrait in pastel, attributed to Gerrit Schipper, ca. 1804. Courtesy of the American Antiquarian Society.

great deal about printing from him. In 1761, when Draper departed, Isaiah was able to do most of the typesetting and assist Fowle with the presswork.

The boy grew into a tall and handsome young man who was well respected among his fellows, both for his courteous manner and for his competence as a printer. At the age of sixteen, Isaiah was running Fowle's shop, and there can be little doubt that the young man had surpassed his master. Just before he reached eighteen he had a serious falling out with Fowle, on September 19, 1765. Oddly enough, Thomas, who was seldom at a want for words, never explained the substance of the dispute, merely characterizing it as a "serious fracas." In any case, Thomas broke his indenture (as had the young Benjamin Franklin some years before) and took ship for Halifax on his way to London. Finding no passage to London, he went to work for Anthony Henry, the town's only printer. Thomas found in Henry a master who was as incompetent and lazy as Fowle. Soon Henry turned the operation of the shop and the publication of the *Halifax Gazette* over to his young journeyman. Thomas brought a new efficiency to the shop, but he also brought his patriot views and used the newspaper to attack the Stamp Act. Within six months Thomas was sacked, and he left Halifax. He spent some time working for different printers in Portsmouth, New Hampshire, and then returned to Boston.

The young man soon headed south to Wilmington, North Carolina, where he unsuccessfully attempted to set up his own press. However, he quickly headed farther south, to Charleston, where he found employment as a journeyman with Robert Wells, the city's finest printer and publisher of the *South Carolina and American General Gazette*. Thomas spent two years in Charleston, finally working in a well-run shop with a competent master. On Christmas Day 1769 he acquired a wife, Mary Dill of Bermuda. It was an unfortunate marriage, as Thomas related (in the third person): "Soon after his marriage to his astonishment he found that his wife had had a bastard son before and that she had been prostituted to the purposes of more than one." They had two children together, but he divorced her in 1777 after many infidelities on her part, in particular after she ran off with Benjamin Thompson, later Count Rumford.

At the age of twenty-one Thomas returned to Boston and in partnership with Fowle launched the *Massachusetts Spy*. Within months Thomas and Fowle quarreled, and Fowle sold out to Thomas. The *Spy* soon became the most successful and important newspaper in New England. Thomas was an ardent patriot, and his newspaper reflected his views. Consequently, he was often in trouble with the authorities. At one point he was charged with libel by Governor Hutchinson, but the suit was dropped. As tensions increased, Thomas packed his press and equipment into a wagon and left Boston. As he put it, he "stole out of town in the dead of night" to set up shop in Worcester. Two nights later Paul Revere spread the alarm, and the following day saw the battles at Lexington and Concord.

The war years were difficult for Thomas. He managed to publish the *Spy* for a year or so but had a quarrel with a local minister who managed to turn Worcester against him. Thomas leased the *Spy* to two other printers (who were unable to make a success of it), and he and his children left Worcester, probably for Londonderry, New Hampshire, though this period is something of a mystery. In the spring of 1778 he returned to Worcester and the *Spy*. On May 26, 1779, Thomas married his cousin Mary and finally found a fulfilling wife and a happy home.

With the end of the war, the *Spy* prospered and provided Thomas with a steady source of revenue, but he began to move in new directions. He decided not to return to Boston and instead remained in Worcester, where he built a fine house and adjoining shop, which housed his original press (still to be seen at the American Antiquarian Society in Worcester), a bindery, the town's post office (during the war Thomas had been appointed postmaster), and what was to be the finest bookshop in the nation.

Now he turned his attention to book publishing. He built his firm on the foundation of the *Spy*, his widely read almanacs, and government publications, such as compilations of state laws. Time and again Thomas took advantage of current events to bring out very profitable bestsellers. For example, at the time of Shays's Rebellion (an armed outbreak by debtor farmers in western Massachusetts in 1786–87) he rushed into print George Minot's *History of the Insurrections in Massachusetts*, which was an instant bestseller.

At about this time, Thomas began to expand both his printing and his bookselling enterprises. He took on many partners, most for less than two years, in a number of cities and towns across the new nation in an effort to create a distribution network. Soon he

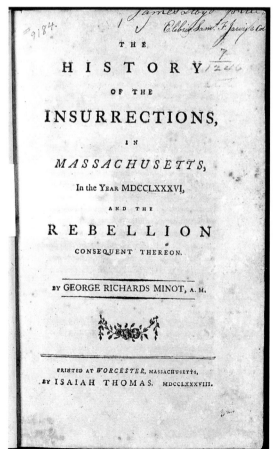

THE

HISTORY

OF THE

INSURRECTIONS,

IN

MASSACHUSETTS,

In the YEAR MDCCLXXXVI,

AND THE

REBELLION

CONSEQUENT THEREON.

BY GEORGE RICHARDS MINOT, A. M.

PRINTED AT *WORCESTER*, MASSACHUSETTS,
BY ISAIAH THOMAS. MDCCLXXXVIII.

In response to a public desire to know more about recent events, Isaiah Thomas was quick to get books such as George Minot's History of the Insurrections in Massachusetts *in print. In 1786 and 1787 Daniel Shays led an insurrection of western Massachusetts farmers who objected to higher land taxes and foreclosures on their mortgages. Minot's account was heavily biased against Shays's Rebellion, but this did not stop eager readers from purchasing copies.*

Noah Webster's American Spelling Book *was one of the nation's all-time bestsellers. Soon after it appeared in 1783, Isaiah Thomas tried to convince Webster to give him exclusive rights to the schoolbook, but it was only after several years that Webster granted Thomas the copyright for Massachusetts and several other states for fourteen very profitable years. Webster's* Spelling Book, *which was distinctly American, standardized and regularized the American version of English, and came to play a fundamental part in American education. Generations of children used the book, and by 1890 sixty million copies had been sold.*

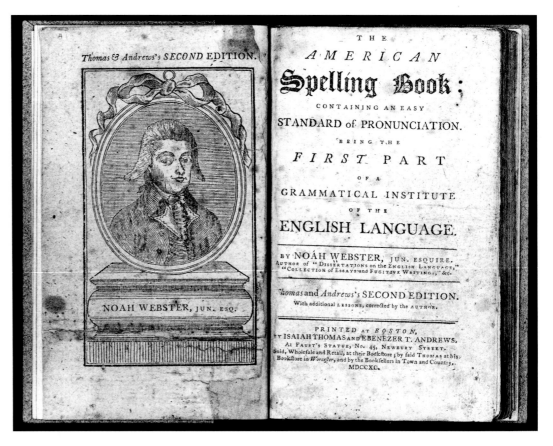

had sixteen presses in operation and five bookstores in Massachusetts, and one each in Albany, Baltimore, and Concord, New Hampshire. Though Worcester was home, and remained the center of his extended enterprises, Thomas's most important business was in Boston, where he reestablished himself in 1788 in partnership with a former apprentice, Ebenezer T. Andrews, as the firm of Thomas and Andrews. Thomas and Andrews soon surpassed Franklin and Hall as the nation's foremost publisher, producing more than four hundred titles during Thomas's lifetime.

Seeing the success of Noah Webster's spelling book, which was first published in 1783, Thomas tried to buy the exclusive rights to it for Massachusetts but failed. Instead, he brought out his own speller, the *New American Spelling Book*, and then another speller by William Perry, both in 1785. Perry's speller was a moderate success but was never able to surpass Webster's. Webster, though, soon offered Thomas the copyright to the speller, and some other titles, for Massachusetts, Rhode Island, and New Hampshire. During the fourteen years of the copyright, Thomas and Andrews sold 300,000 copies of Webster's speller. They brought out thirty editions of that bestseller and six editions of Webster's grammar. These are impressive figures, and in terms of sales such textbooks formed the largest part of the business.

The earliest children's books produced in the American colonies were pious tracts, such as John Cotton's Milk for Babes Drawn Out of the Breasts of Both Testaments *(1646), which were little different from those intended for adults. Children's books intended for leisure reading were introduced to America by the English publisher John Newbery in the middle of the eighteenth century. Isaiah Thomas began publishing such Newbery titles as* Mother Goose *and* Goody Two-Shoes *in 1779 and soon came out with American versions such as this 1787* Goody Two-Shoes.

With textbooks forming such an important part of Thomas and Andrews's list, it was a logical move to develop and exploit the market for children's books. In 1779 Thomas acquired several of Englishman John Newbery's chapbooks for children, which proved to be quite successful in America. He went on to publish other English titles such as *Mother Goose* and *Goody Two-Shoes*. Following this success, he brought out his own American titles, including an American *Mother Goose*. These books were issued in five sizes, the smallest consisted of 32 small pages selling for four cents, and the largest consisted of 104 pages selling for twenty cents. Children's books were so successful that in 1787 nineteen titles were published by Thomas and Andrews. Overall, they published sixty-six titles in 119 editions. Though Thomas was not particularly interested in children's books, it is his introduction of this genre to America for which he is often remembered.

Another significant aspect of the firm's list was Bibles. In 1786 Thomas published an abridged hieroglyphic Bible for children. In 1790 he initiated a grand project for a new Bible, not unlike the project initiated by King James I in the early 1600s. Thomas intended that the new Bible, which had the benefit of the advice and scholarship of a great many American clergymen, would be issued in two formats, a large, deluxe, two-volume set with fifty copperplate engravings and a more modest, one-volume version with fewer illustrations. The first volume of the deluxe set and the single-volume edition were published in December 1791, to a very favorable reception (the

76 JONAH I. *ver.* 15. II. *ver.* 1, 10.

The Mariners took up and caſt him into the Sea, and it ceaſed from raging. Now the LORD had prepared a great to ſwallow up Jonah, and he was in its Belly three Days and three Nights. Then he prayed unto the Lord, and it upon the dry Land.

The Mariners took up *Jonah* and caſt him into the Sea, and it ceaſed from raging. Now the Lord had prepared a great *Fiſh* to ſwallow up Jonah, and he was in its Belly three Days and three Nights. Then he prayed unto the Lord, and it *vomited out Jonah* upon the dry Land.

One of the more unusual of Isaiah Thomas's books for children was his hieroglyphic abridged Bible, first published in 1786. It was intended to assist a child who was not yet ready to read the standard Bible and no doubt found many semi-literate adult readers as well.

second volume of the deluxe set appeared in the next year). In 1793 he published a smaller Bible in one volume, which was also well received. But even before he had completed his large Bible project, he initiated a new project of an extraordinary nature.

Thomas knew that nearly every family in the United States had need of a Bible but that given the expense, families of modest means often saved and suffered great hardships to be able to purchase one. What Thomas proposed was to produce an elegant and affordable Bible that would be within the reach of even the most humble. The Bible was a large book that required a great deal of composition, or typesetting. No American printer had enough type to enable him to set the entire Bible, but instead had to set a few pages, print them, distribute the type back into the cases, set a few more pages, and so forth. Thomas knew that if a publisher had the whole Bible in standing type, he could reprint it again and again at very little cost and great profit. And this is what he intended to accomplish. In 1790 he contracted with a London printer to set the whole Bible in standing type and ship it across the Atlantic to him. The project took six years to complete, mostly because Thomas had trouble raising the £1,144 to pay for the type. Things moved slowly as the finished pages of standing type were periodically shipped to Thomas, but finally in 1797 it was finished. This small inexpensive Bible, known as the Standing Bible, was very popular, and Thomas was able to reprint it as needed from the standing type. It was both profitable for the publisher and a bargain for the purchaser. The easy availability of these Bibles no doubt did much to stimulate reading and increase both the breadth and the depth of literacy among the citizens of the new nation, particularly those spread out along the expanding frontier.

In the mid-1790s Thomas was at the height of his activities as a publisher. He employed about 150 people in Worcester alone. His backlist had great depth in textbooks and Bibles and a range that was unrivaled. He published topical works such as Thomas Paine's *Age of Reason* and novels and works of literature

THE

HOLY BIBLE,

CONTAINING THE

OLD and NEW TESTAMENTS:

TRANSLATED OUT OF THE

Original Tongues,

AND

WITH THE FORMER TRANSLATIONS

DILIGENTLY COMPARED AND REVISED,

BY THE

Special Command of King JAMES I, of *England*.

GENESIS ii. 17.

United States of Columbia.

PRINTED AT WORCESTER, MASSACHUSETTS.
BY ISAIAH THOMAS.
Sold by him in WORCESTER, by Wholesale, Bound or in Sheets.
Sold also by said THOMAS and ANDREWS, in BOSTON, and by the
Booksellers in the UNITED STATES OF COLUMBIA.

1799.

This small, unassuming, and inexpensive Bible, known as the Standing Bible, ultimately brought Isaiah Thomas considerable profit and success. The Standing Bible took about six years to finish and cost the Worcester publisher a sizable sum of money. Thomas wanted to put the whole Bible, one of the best-selling books in America, in standing type so that it could be reprinted at any time without having to be reset again and again. No printer in America had so much type on hand, so he contracted with a London printer who sent the completed pages across the Atlantic as fast as Thomas could find money to pay for them. Finally, in 1797 the Bible was completed. Thomas was able to undercut his competitors and offer the public a good Bible at a bargain price. He used the standing type to reprint the Bible again and again, this copy having been reprinted in 1799. Once he had recovered his initial investment, a large portion of his proceeds from the Bible was profit.

such as Goldsmith's *Vicar of Wakefield*, Sterne's *Sentimental Journey*, and Richardson's *Pamela*. In addition, he continued to issue children's books and inexpensive books intended for the less sophisticated reader, such as *The Amours and Adventures of Two English Gentlemen in Italy*. However, it was the category of works known as "standard authors" that formed the bedrock of his list. These were works such as Jeremy Belknap's *American Biography*, the first American biographical dictionary, and a number of standard medical works and reprints. Further, he specialized in publishing Fourth of July orations and Masonic works. By the end of the century Isaiah Thomas was one of the nation's richest men, with a fortune estimated at over $150,000.

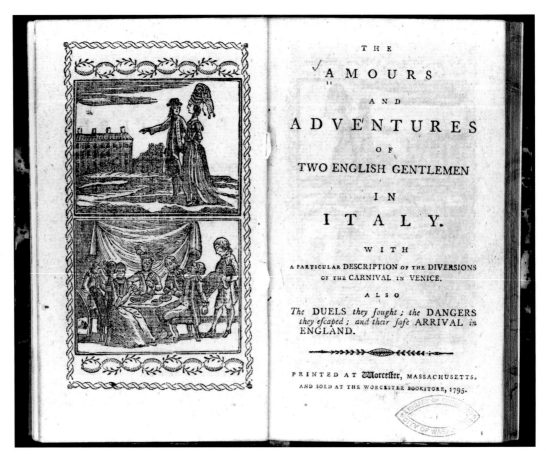

Isaiah Thomas published a wide variety of titles, most of which were serious works such as Webster's American Spelling Book, *the Bible, and novels by authors like Oliver Goldsmith, but he also published works such as* The Amours and Adventures of Two English Gentlemen in Italy, *issued in 1795, for the less sophisticated reader. Such titles often proved more profitable than the works of the established novelists because they were cheaper to produce and sold more copies.*

In 1802 Thomas gradually began to retire and withdraw from his various businesses. He turned over the *Spy* to his son and three years later established him in a bookstore in Springfield, but the younger Thomas found little success. Thomas and some of his partners were dealt a serious blow when their bookstores in Baltimore, Albany, and Walpole were destroyed during the War of 1812. His second wife died in 1818, and his son followed five months later. In 1819 Thomas married his late wife's housekeeper, Rebecca Armstrong, but separated from her in less than three years. In 1820 he ended his partnership with Ebenezer Andrews, thus bringing to an end the firm of Thomas and Andrews. By this time, however, the firm had fallen on hard times, and Thomas realized only $22,000 from the split. He continued to sell property, equipment, and copyrights as his fortune steadily decreased. By 1825 all that remained from his publishing business was his stock of books, which was valued at $39,000.

Though he was the nation's first great publisher, Thomas is more often remembered for two things. The first is his *History of Printing in America*, and the second is the founding of the American Antiquarian Society. In the early 1790s Thomas began collecting examples of early American printing (he purchased a copy of Eliot's In-

The American Antiquarian Society was founded in Worcester, Massachusetts, in 1812 by Isaiah Thomas. Thomas's library, which he had used to write his History of Printing in America, *forms the core of the institution's collection. From the beginning, the scope of the collection was broad and inclusive, especially strong in ephemeral items such as broadsides and pamphlets. After Thomas's death in 1831, successive librarians continued to collect books, newspapers, and other materials produced by American printers. In time the library confined its collecting to the period up to 1876 and has become the preeminent research institution for such materials. In recent years the AAS has been at the forefront of the study of the role of books in society by establishing the Program in the History of the Book in American Culture. Courtesy of the American Antiquarian Society.*

dian Bible for $7) and began bringing together documents relating to the early American book trade. On April 1, 1808, he began his history, a loosely structured narrative containing notes on everything and anything he could uncover or knew firsthand. It was published in 1810 and remains a valuable work to this day. In 1812, together with Aaron Bancroft and Oliver Fiske, Thomas founded the American Society of Antiquaries in Worcester. He was elected the society's first president, an office he held until his death in 1831, and he subsequently gave the society his library and all his papers. This donation formed the nucleus of what has grown into one of the world's premier research libraries, the American Antiquarian Society.

Isaiah Thomas had opened the door and shown the way ahead for the development of modern publishing in America, but it was Matthew Carey of Philadelphia who strode through that door and created the first of the new nineteenth-century publishing houses. The publisher's function has always been present in the book trade, but in the first decades of the century it developed into a separate function. The new publisher acted as a central connection to the various branches of the book trade and coordinated the whole. In the past many of the different functions of

Matthew Carey was America's first modern publisher. A fugitive Irish activist, he landed in Philadelphia aboard the ship America *in 1784. Ten years later he was one of the nation's premier publishers and also one of its greatest debtors. Never far from bankruptcy, he was saved by backing the right party in the election of 1800 and gaining an appointment as a director of the Bank of Pennsylvania, which eased his credit problems considerably. Even so, solvency and profitability came to Carey through the successful piracy of English novelists like Sir Walter Scott and the subscription sales of Bibles and other books by salespeople such as Mason Locke Weems in the hinterlands.*

the trade were carried on by a single individual or firm. Benjamin Franklin is an example of an author who printed his own books, financed them, published them, distributed and sold them, and even read them. Isaiah Thomas also combined the roles of manufacturing, publishing, and distribution, but as the new century progressed, these became distinct and separate businesses. It was the publisher who assumed the most important role: He was the entrepreneur who had vision, who risked capital, who brought together all the pieces, and who directed the process that made the book trade successful. Isaiah Thomas was never a publisher in the full modern sense, though he certainly functioned as a publisher as well as printer and bookseller. Matthew Carey began in the same mold, but long before his retirement in 1824 he had broken the mold and emerged as a modern publisher.

Matthew Carey grew up in Dublin, the son of a businessman. He was a shy and studious youth who taught himself French at an early age. At the age of fifteen, he disagreed with his father as to a future trade. He wanted to become a printer and bookseller, but his father would have none of it. The elder Carey offered his son the choice of twenty-five other trades, but the young man remained obdurate. Without his father's help, Matthew found his own master printer and began to learn the mysteries of the book trade. During these years when he was learning the trade, he also began to write pamphlets and political essays. One of his political pamphlets denounced the British penal system as an instrument designed to subjugate Irish Catholics. Carey urged his compatriots to rebel against the system, and this quite naturally was not well received by the British government. At the same time, a conservative Catholic organization, which might have been expected to support Carey's position against the government, denounced the pamphlet. Carey then branded the organization as "the most servile body in Europe," whereupon it posted a reward for Carey's arrest and initiated a lawsuit against him. With both the British and the Irish at his heels, Carey fled to France.

Carey had the very good luck to find his way to Passy, in the suburbs of Paris, where he obtained employment with Benjamin Franklin, at that time the American minister to France. Franklin had set up a small press to amuse himself by printing dispatches from America. There was not a great deal of printing to occupy Carey, but the young man had the exceptional opportunity to meet a number of influential men. One such was the Marquis de Lafayette, who was very interested in what Carey could tell him of the situation in Ireland. Franklin realized that Carey was gaining little experience with his small press and soon arranged for him to be taken into the large firm of Didot in Paris.

Returning to Dublin after about a year in Paris, Carey set up publishing revolutionary newspapers, in particular the *Volunteers' Journal*, which he began in October 1783. It was immediately successful, but because of that success, Carey was brought before the House of Commons on a criminal libel charge and sentenced to Newgate Prison. After a month in prison he was released, but still facing other charges, he decided to flee the country again. Disguised as a woman, he obtained passage on the ship *America*. Because of his friendship with Franklin, he decided to go to Philadelphia.

Arriving in Philadelphia on November 1, 1784, he soon met Lafayette, who gave him $400 to encourage the young Irishman in his new country. He decided to establish a newspaper and with the money from Lafayette purchased an old press and equipment. On January 25, 1785, the *Pennsylvania Evening Herald* appeared. The *Herald* opposed the political views of the *Independent Gazetteer*, published by Colonel Eleazer Oswald, a staunch Federalist, and the two publishers used their respective newspapers to conduct attacks on each other. In the end Carey was wounded in a duel with Oswald and was forced to retract his assertions (though in time he would become a Federalist himself). He sold the *Herald* in 1788.

Meanwhile, in October 1786, Carey and five partners had launched the *Columbian Magazine*, which was quite successful. Carey was not happy working with so many partners, however, and he withdrew at the end of the year to establish his own magazine, the *American Museum*. It was his intention that the *American Museum* would be a national magazine. However, he was immediately confronted with the problem of getting the magazine out to potential subscribers. He wrote to printers and booksellers across the country to ask them to act as agents, and he traveled up and down the country establishing contacts. Soon subscriptions were flooding into his Philadelphia office. In spite of the large number of subscriptions,

"Never was more labour bestowed on a work, with less reward," was how Matthew Carey characterized his efforts on the American Museum. *Founded by Carey in 1787, the monthly magazine flourished for a time and included both original and reprinted contributions, such as this intriguing treatise on how the printer should "adapt the size of his types to the spirit of the author … ." Carey developed a wide network of contacts through all the states to distribute and sell the magazine, but in spite of his Herculean efforts the magazine was barely profitable. With the increase in postal rates in 1792, the* American Museum *ceased publication.*

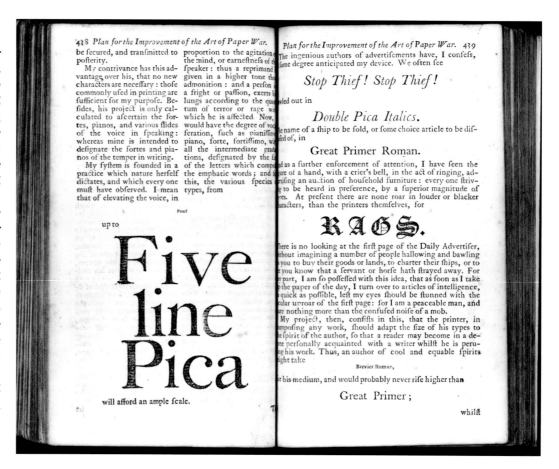

he was plagued by the costs of distributing the magazine. Delays were common, the roads nearly nonexistent, shipments were lost, and agents were unable to collect payments. As Carey put it, "Never was more labour bestowed on a work, with less reward." In 1792 Congress raised the postage rates for magazines, and any hope of profitability vanished. The *Museum* ceased publication. Nonetheless, the magazine gave Carey a national reputation, both with the general public and within the book trade.

Carey first began printing books in 1785, but his first major publication was the Douay Bible in 1790. This standard English translation of the Catholic Vulgate was well received and sold well. In 1792, with no capital of his own, Carey established a bookshop and became a major wholesaler of books imported from Britain based on credit advanced by British publishers. As with the *Museum*, the major problem he faced was how to get books out to the booksellers and other retailers. This conundrum has faced the American printer, publisher, and bookseller from the earliest days and has continued to bedevil the book trade down to the present day.

Making a book has always been a relatively straightforward process, but marketing and distributing it across vast geographical distances to a sparsely populated nation presented problems as large as the country. The book trade was fragmented into many geographical parts, some larger and some smaller, but generally functioning in isolation. The least fragmented parts of this puzzle were in the older cities of Boston, New York, and Philadelphia, but many regional centers existed in such towns as Hartford, Connecticut; Brattleboro, Vermont; Burlington, New Jersey; Pittsburgh, Reading, Lancaster, and Germantown, Pennsylvania; Cincinnati, Ohio; Dumfries, Virginia; and Whitehall, North Carolina, among others. Printers and booksellers in these towns tried to serve a relatively large geographical region, but the problem of transporting goods was a serious one. Transportation on water was cheaper than by land, but the great rivers were navigable only so far inland. Land transportation over virtually nonexistent roads was a nightmare. Because of these difficulties the regional centers had developed, and each printer had staked out a natural territory defined by the limits imposed by profitable transportation. But this solution created other problems. No single printer, or group of printers, located in a regional center could supply the wide range of books and publications required by an increasingly literate and demanding reading public. What each bookseller in each center needed was a few copies of many different books, rather than many copies of a few titles.

Carey's solution to the fragmentary centers was to promote a system of exchange, whereby each printer or bookseller could exchange a certain quantity of his own books for a similar quantity of another's books. This allowed each bookseller to have a wide range of titles—theoretically each bookseller would be able to offer the full range of books published in both America and Britain—and it discouraged publishers in different regions from bringing out redundant titles. In effect, it was the beginning of a national book trade connected through a web of coordinated regional centers. Carey's wholesale British books were first offered to the same booksellers who had acted for him when he published the *Museum* and in time included many others. The larger booksellers often exchanged titles in their own stock with Carey's offerings, but the smaller booksellers more often purchased Carey's books at a discount or took them on consignment at a $12\frac{1}{2}$ percent commission. This business expansion was financed entirely on credit, and though it generated a huge cash flow (it is estimated that $300,000 passed through Carey's hands during the 1790s), it created very little profit for Carey, as almost all his cash went to his creditors.

In 1794 and 1795 Carey greatly expanded his publishing activities. In these two years he published over sixty books and pamphlets, a total equal to his entire previous output. Foremost among these new titles were two large luxury works, which he brought out at great risk. Up until this time such large works were generally published only in London, the American bookseller importing a few copies for what

In the mid-1790s Matthew Carey brought out two deluxe publications of a kind heretofore rarely attempted in America. These were William Guthrie's New System of Modern Geography *and Oliver Goldsmith's* History of the Earth and Animated Nature. *Each of these large multivolume works included numerous engraved plates, such as the armillary sphere in Guthrie's* Geography *and the lion in Goldsmith's* Animated Nature. *In addition, Guthrie's* Geography *included a separate atlas composed of about fifty large engraved maps. Though Carey demonstrated that the American book trade was capable of producing deluxe books, he found himself unable to market the expensive sets. He was rescued by the arrival of Mason Locke Weems, who first suggested a plan to sell books by subscription as the two men sat round a table in Carey's back room surrounded by piles of unsold books.*

was perceived to be a limited trade. Carey ventured to believe that there was a large American market for such works that could be exploited by an American publisher. The first of these works was William Guthrie's *New System of Modern Geography*, two volumes with an atlas of about fifty large engraved maps, in an edition of twenty-five hundred copies selling at $12 (later $16) per set. The second was Oliver Goldsmith's *History of the Earth and Animated Nature*, four volumes with fifty-five plates, in an edition of three thousand copies selling at $6 (later $10) per set. In the midst of this expansion, just after he finished Guthrie's *Geography*, Carey sold his printing shop and contracted out all his printing. He was the first American publisher to lay aside his identity as printer and assume the role of a modern publisher.

Carey found himself confronted with a vast debt that was extended to the limit in 1796. He owed huge sums to British publishers, American bankers, local printers, papermakers, binders, and others. True, he was selling an ever increasing number of books, but even a slight downward fluctuation in his income could spell bankruptcy. In the face of this debt, he cut back his publishing to almost nothing and solicited subscriptions for already published works through his established network. But his network was cumbersome and could not bear much more traffic. He needed to look elsewhere to sell books on a scale never before witnessed in America.

Carey's savior was a most unlikely figure, Mason Locke Weems, popularly known as Parson Weems, who combined the spellbinding righteousness of a proselytizing preacher with the persuasive skills of the most successful itinerant salesman. Weems is best known today for his biography of George Washington, a work that was extremely successful, both financially and in shaping the nation's perception of its first president. The story of Washington and the cherry tree was Weems's creation, and in spite of all attempts to dislodge it from the nation's psyche, it endures. Carey and Weems first met in Philadelphia in the winter of 1795. Carey showed Weems his back room containing nearly three thousand copies of Goldsmith's *Animated Nature* that he had been unable to move. Weems sat down and sketched a brilliant prospectus for the work, which, as he recounted later, "gave the people to expect that 'worlds on worlds inclosed were to burst upon their senses,' if they would but seize the precious moment to subscribe to this marvelous book." With such inspired salesmanship, Weems set forth into Lancaster County to obtain subscriptions for Goldsmith and the atlas that accompanied Guthrie's *Geography*. Soon he had a contract from Carey giving him the territory of Virginia and Maryland and 25 percent of all he sold. Within one month he had almost a thousand subscriptions. Weems was enthusiastic about his territory:

One of the greatest book salesmen of all times, Mason Locke Weems sold books for Matthew Carey for about thirty years until his death in 1825. An ordained minister, Parson Weems was a familiar figure along the primitive roads of the backwoods American South who combined the spellbinding righteousness of a proselytizing preacher with the persuasive skills of the most successful itinerant salesman. Weems knew what the common reader wanted: cheap, popular books. After finally convincing Carey that such books would be marketable and profitable, Weems sold tens of thousands and in large measure brought Carey back from the brink of bankruptcy. Portrait from Evart A. Duyckinck's Cyclopaedia of American Literature *(1877).*

> This country is large, and numerous are its inhabitants; to cultivate among these a taste for reading, and by the reflection of proper books to throw far and wide the rays of useful arts and sciences, were at once the work of a true Philanthropist and prudent speculator. For I am verily assured that under proper culture, every dollar that you shall scatter on the field of this experiment will yield you 30, 60, and 100 fold.

Weems is a legendary figure who must have cut quite a figure on the road. Van Wyck Brooks's description, though perhaps overly romantic, still captures something of the essence of Weems on the road.

This "ragged Mother Carey's chicken," as Parson Weems called himself, was a familiar figure on the roads of the South. With his ruddy visage and the locks that flowed over his clerical coat, one saw him bumping along in his jersey wagon, a portable bookcase behind and a fiddle beside him. A little ink-horn hung from one of his lapels, and he carried a quill pen stuck in his hat. … He was abroad in all weathers and all over the country, mostly south of Philadelphia, in Maryland, Virginia, the Carolinas and Georgia,— though he also traveled through New Jersey, as far as New York,—selling Matthew Carey's publications, "beating up the headquarters of all the good old planters and farmers," regardless of blizzards, mosquitoes, floods and fatigue. "Roads horrid and suns torrid" were all the same to Parson Weems; and even when Russian bears were glad to tree themselves he was still glad to sell books, though he had to plough through Virginia runs that all but covered his wagon-wheels, wet, cold, feverish and hungry …

Even the most charismatic salesman could not achieve such a level of success without a system, and Weems was no exception. He styled himself "general," and when he came to a new town he would find a likely associate whom he styled "adjutant." During his stay in a town, he first distributed prospectuses, showed off copies of sample volumes, and delivered sales pitches to all who would listen. In the course of a day or two he would collect a good number of subscriptions. He would then leave prospectuses and perhaps a sample volume with his adjutant, often a store-keeper or postmaster, who could then canvas for further subscriptions. For his efforts, the adjutant typically received one copy in every six or seven that he could sell for himself.

Weems was almost single-handedly opening up new markets in the hinterlands. This extension of Carey's network had the potential finally to solve the publisher's credit problems and enable him to pay off his many debts. Unfortunately, the network was so convoluted, spread over such a wide area, included so many middlemen in remote parts, that cash, in far smaller quantities than he had anticipated, found its way only very slowly into Carey's hands. His response was to work directly with some of the adjutants, rather than through Weems, thus enabling payments to reach him in a timely manner. Further, he reduced the number of adjutants and agents, some of whom had in effect set up branch bookshops, to those who were the most profitable. By 1800 he had a responsive network in place.

During this time when he was refining his network, Carey was also developing his list. He was exchanging large numbers of Guthrie and Goldsmith for other titles that Weems could sell. Weems, however, was not impressed. He regarded these new acquisitions, for example, William Burkitt's *Expository Notes on the New Testament*, or Captain James Cook's *Voyages*, or the *Laws of the United States*, as extraordinarily dull and ponderous works that had no appeal to the rural folk he traveled among. Time and time again he told Carey that the people wanted cheap books of a popular nature. These readers, who were stymied in the limited availability of popular titles, were present in large numbers but spread across the vast distances of the frontier. The profit margin might be quite slim for such popular titles, but Weems knew he could sell thousands of them. By 1797 Carey began to heed Weems's advice and changed his publishing to

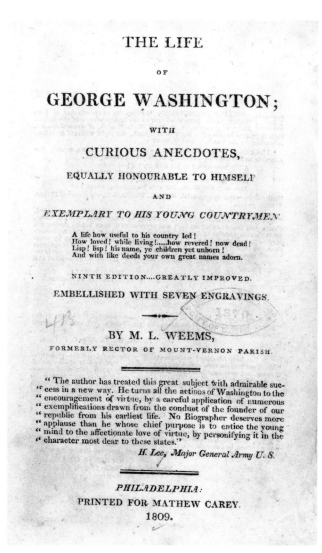

THE LIFE

OF

GEORGE WASHINGTON;

WITH

CURIOUS ANECDOTES,

EQUALLY HONOURABLE TO HIMSELF

AND

EXEMPLARY TO HIS YOUNG COUNTRYMEN.

A life how useful to his country led !
How loved ! while living !.....how revered ! now dead !
Lisp ! lisp ! his name, ye children yet unborn !
And with like deeds your own great names adorn.

NINTH EDITION....GREATLY IMPROVED.

EMBELLISHED WITH SEVEN ENGRAVINGS.

BY M. L. WEEMS,

FORMERLY RECTOR OF MOUNT-VERNON PARISH.

" The author has treated this great subject with admirable suc-
" cess in a new way. He turns all the actions of Washington to the
" encouragement of virtue, by a careful application of numerous
" exemplifications drawn from the conduct of the founder of our
" republic from his earliest life. No Biographer deserves more
" applause than he whose chief purpose is to entice the young
" mind to the affectionate love of virtue, by personifying it in the
" character most dear to these states."

H. Lee, *Major General Army U. S.*

PHILADELPHIA:
PRINTED FOR MATHEW CAREY.
1809.

Mason Locke Weems's Life of George Washington, *first published in 1800, is arguably one of the most influential biographies ever written. In his portrait of Washington as a paragon of virtue, religious principle, patriotism, and justice, Weems single-handedly transformed Washington into the Father of His Country. Weems invented the most famous episode in Washington's life, still known to every American school child, the tale of young George and the cherry tree. In the story, which first appeared in the fifth edition in 1806, George admitted to his father: "I can't tell a lie, Pa; you know I can't tell a lie. I did cut it with my hatchet." Whatever historians may think of the accuracy of Weems's portrait, the American nation has taken it to heart by naming one state, eight waterways, ten lakes, thirty-three counties, nine colleges and universities, and 121 towns in Washington's honor.*

include some inexpensive popular titles; soon his profits increased. The editions of Guthrie and Goldsmith were finally all sold by 1799, Weems having sold half of them, but they had generated more debt than profit. Even with the increase in income from his cheap works, Carey found himself on the edge of financial ruin. The end seemed near when he placed the following advertisement in the *Pennsylvania Gazette* on January 22, 1799:

Books Selling Very Cheap. MATTHEW CAREY, Proposing to quit the Book Selling business, offers his large and valuable Collection of Books for sale, by retail, at a discount of 12 and an 1-2 per cent. from the usual prices. Those who purchase considerable quantities, shall have a further discount.

Carey broke with the Federalists in the late 1790s and supported Thomas Jefferson for the presidency, and when Jefferson assumed office in 1801, Carey was rewarded by an appointment as a director of the Bank of Pennsylvania. As he explained, his new position "afforded considerable facility for meeting my engagements. My debts rose extravagantly high, and … I was treated with great lenity by the Directors, who allowed my notes to run on, without curtailment. …" Bankruptcy had been averted, but Carey was not such a fool as to believe that this seemingly unlimited extension of credit would solve his problems. It allowed him time, however, to revamp his business and network and make them profitable. His major problem was that his debt was too large and had to be reduced. To reduce his debt he needed to increase his profit margin, reduce the number of middlemen in his network, publish titles that would sell in quantity, and sell more books for cash and fewer on consignment.

Weems had long suggested that Carey should publish a large family Bible and contended that he could sell huge quantities at great profit: He characterized it as "a vein of Potosi [the fabulously wealthy Mexican silver mine] to your purse." Carey sent Weems north into New Jersey and New York to gather subscriptions—this time prepaid—for a proposed family Bible. Weems returned to Philadelphia with hundreds of subscriptions and then headed south, where he gathered hundreds more. The Bible was finished in November 1801 and was immediately successful. Weems was responsible for half of the edition of two thousand copies, and other publishers took many on exchange. Within a year the edition had sold out at a substantial profit to Carey. In 1802 he printed two more editions, and in 1803, like Isaiah Thomas, he arranged for the Bible to be set in standing type so that he could reprint it on demand. He printed a new edition of the Bible from the standing type every year thereafter until 1820, and in so doing he paid off his debt and became a rich man. He had at last found his bestseller, he had pruned his network into an effective distribution system, he had established solid exchanges with reputable publishers across the nation, and finally he had let Weems loose in the rural South collecting prepaid subscriptions for cheap, popular works. Another significant source of steady profit for Carey was the reprinting of British novelists such as Sir Walter Scott, who were extraordinarily popular in America.

Carey's promotion of the exchange system began the process of bringing the trade together into what, in the not-too-distant future, would be a true national industry. In December 1801 he invited the booksellers and publishers of America to meet in New York on June 1, 1802. The purpose of the meeting, analogous to the great European book fairs of Frankfurt and Leipzig, was to provide a venue for members of the trade to interact and exchange, sell, and buy books. At the meeting Carey presented the group with a proposed constitution, and the American Company of Booksellers was formed. Hugh Gaine of New York, the nation's oldest bookseller, was elected president. The organization continued for only a few years, as the major publishers withdrew in protest against inland publishers who were using the organization's exchange system to market cheap editions of standard works to the great disadvantage of the established publishers. Carey was also involved in the short-lived New York Association of Booksellers, which also organized in 1802. This organization, which was formed to protect the trade from cheap imports, also soon fell apart. Nearly a century would pass before a viable organization of booksellers was permanently established.

Though Carey failed in creating a national organization for the book trade, in fact he laid the foundation for a truly national trade. He pointed the way ahead by thinking in a grand national style, and though it nearly bankrupted him, he persevered, and in the end his network linked all the major publishers and booksellers. Once these previously disparate and fragmented elements of the book trade were connected, even if only at an informal level, there could be no turning back to the isolation of the past. This achievement is Carey's greatest legacy, and for his vision he has justly been called the first modern publisher in America.

The Boston Public Library, which opened in 1854, was the prototype American public library. Financed as a municipal institution by taxation specified for that purpose, it offered free admission to all, circulating books that could be removed from the library, and a range of resources that were freely available. In 1870 it opened the first branch library in the country. The Boston Public Library's magnificent "Place for the People," with its Renaissance grandeur and American murals, opened in 1895. The Boston Public Library's collections have grown to include over six million books, making it one of the nation's most significant research libraries, but it continues to maintain the democratic ideal of public service that was such an important part of its foundation. Photographs for the Detroit Publishing Co., ca. 1900, by William Henry Jackson.

Libraries in America

"I have often thought that nothing would do more extensive good at small expense than the establishment of a small circulating library in every county."

—Thomas Jefferson

ibraries have been part of American culture from the very beginning, in the private collections of individuals, colleges, and organizations. Though the origins of the public library in America can be traced to Benjamin Franklin's Library Company of Philadelphia in the eighteenth century and to the foundation of similar private institutions such as the Boston Athenaeum in the nineteenth century, the public library as a free institution supported by dedicated tax revenues dates to 1854 and the Boston Public Library. Jefferson's prescient desire to see a library in each community became a reality in the second half of the nineteenth century and the first part of the twentieth. Influenced by the example of the Boston Public Library and by the Public Library Movement in Britain, communities across the nation established public libraries, so that by 1875 there were 257 public libraries. But the greatest impetus for the establishment of public libraries came from Andrew Carnegie's vision of the library as an educational agent for the public good.

The Boston Athenaeum opened in 1806 as a reading room for the Anthology Society. With a charter membership of 150, dues were used not only to purchase books and maintain the reading room, but also to establish lecture series and an educational program. Many other American cities emulated the Boston Athenaeum and created similar institutions that combined books and culture. Photograph by Charles H. Currier, ca. 1895.

Andrew Carnegie, born in Scotland, emigrated to America with his family in 1848. By the 1870s he was well on his way to becoming one of the nation's key industrialists. In his Gospel of Wealth, *which was published as a book in 1900, he asserted that the rich were trustees for the public good. In the next year he sold his industrial interests to J. P. Morgan and put his belief into practice by endowing such educational institutions as the Carnegie Institute (now Carnegie-Mellon University) and establishing a fund to build libraries in communities across the nation. These libraries, known as Carnegie libraries, brought reading and books to all parts of the country and to people who had never had ready access to literature.*

Opened on May 18, 1909, at a cost of $2,500, the Carnegie Public Library in Parsons, Kansas, was similar to many hundreds of such libraries built across the country. The library, seen here in about 1920, served the community well for many decades, but in 1977, as in many other communities, a new library was built to replace it. The Carnegie building was saved from demolition, however, and converted into a civic building that continues to serve the city's cultural needs. Courtesy of the Kansas Collection, Kenneth Spencer Research Library, University of Kansas.

*Newspaper reading room of
the Omaha, Nebraska, Public
Library. Photograph by John
Vachon for the Farm Security
Administration, November
1938.*

Academic Libraries

Books have always played a central role in colleges and universities, whether in libraries, bookstores, or student rooms. Until the end of the nineteenth century, academic institutions in the United States relied on small library collections and students used standard textbooks, but with an expansion of undergraduate education, involving a multiplicity of offerings, and a new emphasis on graduate education and research, academic libraries began to grow at an unprecedented rate that continues to this day. Campus bookstores also expanded, offering thousands of titles beyond the stock textbooks, and library book sales were eagerly anticipated by students and faculty anxious for a bargain.

When the University of Kansas opened in 1866, it had only three professors and one of the many things lacking was a library. A little more than twenty years later, the University occupied a large building (later known as Fraser Hall) that included a well-appointed library, pictured here. The University's first librarian, Carrie Watson, assumed her position in 1887, and she can be seen behind the desk at the right rear. Courtesy of the University Archives, Kenneth Spencer Research Library, University of Kansas.

Named for the University of Kansas's first librarian, Watson Library was completed in 1924. It contained about 184,000 volumes and could accommodate eight hundred students. Following World War II, the University entered a period of unprecedented prosperity, and library collections grew at a rapid pace. Watson Library was expanded and renovated several times, including the creation of an undergraduate library (pictured here in 1955), an innovative approach that catered to the specific needs of undergraduates. The Lamont Library at Harvard (1949) was the first separate undergraduate library and served as a model for academic libraries across the country. Courtesy of the University Archives, Kenneth Spencer Research Library, University of Kansas.

Although libraries traditionally place great emphasis on the acquisition of books, a lesser known function is the disposition of books. Often libraries receive donations that include titles already held by the library and titles outside the collecting scope of the institution. These books are often offered for sale, the proceeds being used to purchase other books for the library. Academic libraries exist in a literate and bibliophilic community whose members eagerly await such library book sales as the one pictured here in 1960 at the University of Kansas. Courtesy of the University Archives, Kenneth Spencer Research Library, University of Kansas.

The Newberry Library in Chicago, one of the world's foremost private research libraries, was founded in 1887 as a result of a bequest from businessman Walter Loomis Newberry. Under the direction of its first librarian, William Frederick Poole, an innovative Romanesque building was constructed in 1893 that emphasized a decentralized structure of separate subject reading rooms and the effective use of natural light. As a result of a cooperative agreement with the John Crerar Library and the Chicago Public Library, the Newberry Library established its particular mission as a research library for the humanities. With collections numbered at 1.5 million printed volumes and 5 million manuscripts, the Newberry Library's greatest strengths lie in western Europe from the Middle Ages to the Napoleonic period, and the Americas from the period of the explorations to the twentieth century. Photograph for the Detroit Publishing Co., ca. 1901.

The Harper brothers, Fletcher, James, John, and Wesley, created what would eventually become the world's largest publishing house and a firm that endures to this day. The Harpers were quick to adopt new technologies, such as power presses, stereotyping, and cloth bindings. The brothers also were at the forefront in the development of new marketing techniques, which, together with the emphasis on new technologies, very soon raised the House of Harper from obscurity to a position of primacy among the New York publishing houses in the 1820s and national dominance by mid-century. Halftone from Harper's Magazine, *1863.*

III
The Rise of the Great Houses
1821–1865

t the turn of the century Philadelphia was the center of the book trade, due in no small part to Matthew Carey and Benjamin Franklin before him, but Boston and New York were also significant centers. The network of printers and booksellers from the largest publisher to the most insignificant itinerant salesman was anchored in these great coastal cities. Even with Carey's retirement from the trade in 1824, Philadelphia managed to maintain its position for another decade or so as Matthew's son, Henry, tenaciously battled the upstart New York houses. But by the time of Henry's retirement in 1838, New York had surpassed Philadelphia as the nation's publishing center. New York was positioned geographically in such a way that greatly favored trade, both from Europe and into the interior. New York was typically the first landing for ships making the transatlantic crossing, and thus the city received news, new books, and talented immigrants first. The Hudson River provided easy water-borne transportation into the interior, and with the development of the Erie Canal system, New York became the gateway to the West. With its geographic assets and its booming and dynamic population, New York was poised to become the commercial center of the United States.

New York witnessed the establishment of a number of great publishing houses in this period. The first was J.&J. Harper in 1817, followed by Appleton in 1825, D.G. Francis in 1826, Van Nostrand & White in 1830, John Wiley & Sons in 1832, John F. Trowe in 1836, Wiley, Long & Putnam in 1836, Dodd, Mead & Co. in 1839, A.S. Barnes & Co. in 1845, Charles Scribner in 1845, and Edward P. Dutton in 1852. But it was the oldest house, that of the brothers Harper, that set the standard and continued to lead the book trade for many decades. The two oldest brothers, James and John, established a printing shop in New York in 1817, at first engaging in odd-job printing but soon expanding into book printing, though at this point, still for other publishers. Finding business slow, the Harpers decided to publish something on their own. In 1818 they hit upon a scheme to publish Locke's *Essay Concerning Human Understanding* at very little risk. They went round to a number of New York booksellers, showed each a proof copy of the book, and offered to put the bookseller's name on the title page if he would take a minimum of one hundred copies. This scheme proved to be so successful that the Harpers continued it for some years.

Even with the moderate success that such innovative marketing brought, it was the ability to master new technology that quickly thrust the house of Harper to the forefront of New York publishers. Printers and publishers had long desired some simple way of keeping a book in standing type. Isaiah Thomas and Matthew Carey, among others, had invested large sums in acquiring whole books set in standing type, but these were exceptional cases. Since the early eighteenth century, experimenters had been trying to create metal plates from impressions or molds made from type set in the normal fashion, so that a book could be easily reprinted from plates rather than the type having to be reset each time. By the early 1820s this process, known as stereotyping, had become a viable technology. Though the typographical purist might decry the subtle loss of definition in a stereotyped book, the use of stereotyped plates enabled publishers to produce books, particularly subsequent editions, quickly and cheaply. The Harper brothers, joined by younger brothers Wesley in 1823 and Fletcher in 1825, quickly adopted the new technique and mastered it to the point that they soon became known as the best book producers in New York. As a result of increasing business, the firm moved three times, finally, in 1825, settling into 82 Cliff Street, a four-story building that now housed the city's largest printing plant.

The Harper brothers were innovators, both in the quick adoption of new technology and in developing new marketing techniques. They were the first in America to issue a book in a cloth binding, and they were among the first American publishers to issue series of books in "libraries." The successful application of cloth to the binding process meant that publishers could now offer the public bound books at very little extra cost. Publisher's bindings in the past had been either temporary paper or pasteboard covers (which would be replaced when the book's owner had it bound at his own expense) or a full leather binding that added considerable cost to the book. With the new technology of cloth binding, a publisher could bind an entire edition, thus placing a finished book in the reader's hands. Cloth bindings became the norm, as consumers quickly came to expect to purchase bound books. These inexpensive cloth bindings were ideal for the Harper series of libraries. The first of these series was the Harper's Family Library, which began publication in 1830. A distinguished editorial board was established, comprising "several gentlemen of high literary acquirements and correct taste … [so that readers might] rest assured that no works will be published by J.&J. Harper but as are interesting, instructive, and moral." The Family Library was generally non-fiction, concentrating in biography, history, and travel. At forty-five cents each, the volumes were priced to sell, which they did with great success. The Family Library continued for fifteen years and included 187 volumes in all. Harper also initiated the Library of Select Novels in 1830 (suspended between 1834 and 1842), the Classical Library and the Boy's and Girl's Library in 1831, and the School District Library in 1841. The School District Library

Henry Carey took over the publishing house his father had established in Philadelphia when Matthew Carey retired in 1824. The firm of Carey & Lea (later Carey, Lea & Blanchard) was the nation's premier publisher, publishing Washington Irving, James Fenimore Cooper, and many of the great English novelists. Carey had a difficult time in beating back the upstart Harper brothers and a host of New York and Boston publishers, but he managed to maintain the firm's position and reputation in the face of fierce competition up until his retirement in 1838. With Henry Carey's departure, the firm was no longer able to maintain its position, and the center of American publishing passed to New York.

was established when the state of New York appropriated funds to establish school district libraries, and the series was created to meet the needs of these new libraries. This was typical of the firm's foresight in seeing an opportunity and business acumen in seizing it: These ready-made libraries, which eventually totaled 295 titles, were very successfully marketed to the school districts of New York and beyond.

Publishers were reevaluating their lists. Typically it might take years to sell the whole run of a particular title, especially of stock or standard works. This tied up capital and reduced the profits to be made from such titles. In the early 1830s, Henry Carey ascertained that "five-sixths of the whole sales are of books manufactured within the year." In 1831 his firm cut back on its stock books and began to concentrate on popular works that would sell immediately, books such as novels, romances, biographies, travel accounts, and so forth. In spite of having reduced the number of stock books issued in 1831, the firm increased its total output by more than 50 percent over the previous year. In addition, the average edition run was increased from 500–750 in 1826 to 1,000–2,000 in the 1830s (and editions of popular novels could be much larger). Extending the runs of editions significantly lowered the unit cost of each book, more so than any technological innovations of the time, and as long as a

James Fenimore Cooper had originally approached New York publisher Charles Wiley in the hope that he might be interested in the then-unknown author's novel, The Spy. Wiley was uninterested, but after the success of the work, the publisher was more than interested in Cooper's subsequent works. Cooper, however, decided to act as his own publisher, as indeed did Washington Irving. Henry Carey pursued both authors with little initial success, but in 1825 Cooper agreed to let Carey & Lea publish his works. One of his greatest successes was The Last of the Mohicans, which was published in 1826. In 1828, Irving also capitulated and became one of Carey's authors. Thus by the end of the 1820s Carey had the two greatest American novelists among his authors, an accomplishment that caused no little jealousy among his fellow publishers.

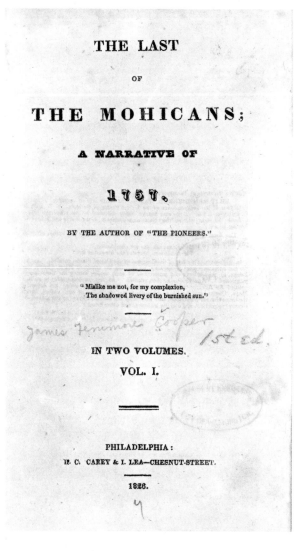

THE LAST

OF

THE MOHICANS;

A NARRATIVE OF

1757.

BY THE AUTHOR OF "THE PIONEERS."

" Mislike me not, for my complexion,
The shadowed livery of the burnished sun."

IN TWO VOLUMES.

VOL. I.

PHILADELPHIA:
H. C. CAREY & I. LEA—CHESNUT-STREET.

1826.

Ralph Waldo Emerson's first collection of essays established his reputation in the United States and abroad when it was published in 1841. His philosophy, rooted in the Puritan inheritance of New England, emphasized individualism, self-reliance, optimism, and hope and has had a profound effect in shaping our national character.

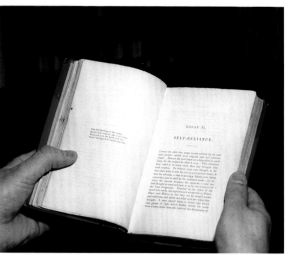

publisher could market these larger quantities, substantial profits were assured. Other firms followed suit, and as a result American publishers were producing more titles in larger numbers and selling them faster than ever. The 1830s also saw a swing away from British to American authors. In 1834 only ten American novels appeared, but in 1835 thirty-one were published. In that year American authors outnumbered foreign authors in every field except fiction (and almost that), poetry, and history. By 1840, 55 percent of the books published in America were by American authors, as compared to 30 percent in 1820.

In 1833 Harper & Bros., as the firm was now known, installed a steam-driven press, one of the first in New York. The old horse that had provided the power for the previous presses was retired to a farm, where he continued to walk in circles, as he had when he walked round and round turning the belts for the Harper presses, unable to break with his old routine. The new printing press was yet another instance of the firm's quick adoption of new breakthroughs in the mechanization of the trade. The year 1833 also saw the beginning of a crisis that was to strain American business, and particularly publishing, to the breaking point. In September

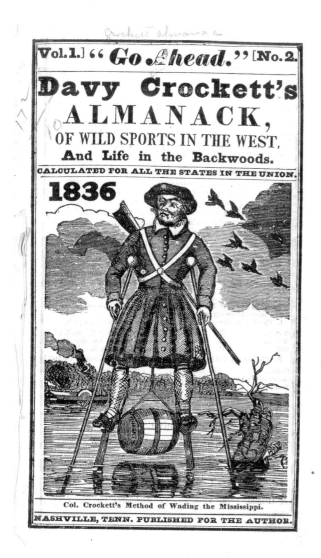

Vol. 1.] "*Go Ahead.*" **[No. 2.**

Davy Crockett's ALMANACK,

OF WILD SPORTS IN THE WEST, And Life in the Backwoods.

CALCULATED FOR ALL THE STATES IN THE UNION.

1836

Col. Crockett's Method of Wading the Mississippi.

NASHVILLE, TENN. PUBLISHED FOR THE AUTHOR.

Davy Crockett was born in 1786 in east Tennessee. In 1811 his family moved west, eventually ending up in the west Tennessee woodlands with which his name later became associated. Crockett hunted, and he fought Indians under Andrew Jackson in 1813–1814. In 1821 he was elected to the state legislature and served in Congress from 1827 to 1831 and again from 1833 to 1835. Defeated in the next election because of his rejection of Jackson and his adoption by the Whigs, he went to Texas to fight against Mexico, dying at the siege of the Alamo in 1836. Though Davy Crockett's life was not dissimilar to that of other backwoods politicians, he embued it with a mythic quality that continued and grew especially after his death. An English observer noted in 1839 that "democracy and the far-west made Colonel Crockett. He is a product of forests, freedom, universal suffrage, and bear-hunts." Crockett was a story teller, and stories were a vital part of his political success. He would capture his listeners' attention, relax them with a good yarn, and then drive home the moral. It was a technique put to good use some years later by another backwoods politician, Abraham Lincoln. Crockett's repertoire of stories was first published in 1834 in the heat of his rejection of Jackson and adoption by the Whigs, as The Life and Adventures of Colonel David Crockett of West Tennessee. *Various Whig politicians and journalists turned out similar books, attributed to Crockett, that built him up as a frontier hero in the hope of attracting votes to the Whig cause. Though the Whigs failed abysmally and Crockett was rejected, the mythic character of Davy Crockett grew larger than ever. One of the publications that first appeared at that time,* Davy Crockett's Almanack, *flourished until about 1856. The* Almanack *featured tall tales concerned with Crockett and others such as Daniel Boone, Kit Carson, and Mike Fink and was largely responsible for the enduring myth of Davy Crockett, a myth that has been retold in the twentieth century through film and television and continues to endure.*

President Andrew Jackson instructed the Treasury Department to transfer public funds from the Bank of the United States to several state banks. As the Bank of the United States contracted its loans, a whole series of bankruptcies ensued, including the well-known publishing house of Collins & Hannay. Cash was hard to come by, and all the publishing houses were finding it harder and harder to meet their obligations. Booksellers were even harder hit, and many went under, which naturally affected the publishers, as they were able to sell fewer books.

As if this were not enough, an internal crisis within the book trade further threatened to diminish profits. The United States had never accepted any form of international copyright, and it had been a long-established custom for American publishers to pirate the works of British authors, who generally received no compensation. This practice had been one of the elements that enabled Matthew Carey to become

William McGuffey, born in Pennsylvania in 1800, spent much of his life in Ohio as a teacher and professor. In the 1830s he began his educational schoolbook series, McGuffey's Eclectic Readers. *Each of the six books endeavored to teach students to read by introducing them to American moral texts and verses such as "Hiawatha" or the "Ride of Paul Revere" and selections from the great English authors. Over 125 million copies of the* Readers *were sold in over two hundred editions. Generations of American school children grew up with the McGuffey series, and many made its moral values their own, thus making McGuffey an integral part of the American experience.*

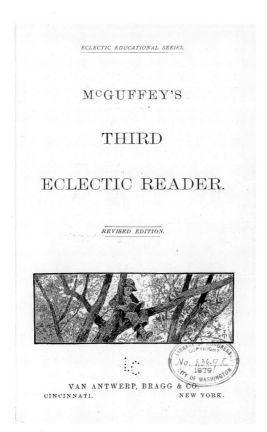

ECLECTIC EDUCATIONAL SERIES.

MᶜGUFFEY'S

THIRD

ECLECTIC READER.

REVISED EDITION.

VAN ANTWERP, BRAGG & CO.
CINCINNATI.   NEW YORK.

the nation's most successful publisher in the preceding generation, and this was not lost on the Harper brothers. In time the two principal rivals for these pirated works were Carey, Lea & Blanchard (as the house of Carey was now known) and Harper & Bros. This rivalry has produced some of the most engaging images of the rough-and-tumble world of American publishing in these early years. British authors such as Sir Walter Scott, and later on Charles Dickens, were immensely popular in the United States, and the American publisher who could get a popular author's next novel in print first was sure to reap great profits. In the case of Sir Walter Scott's *Peveril of the Peak*, Carey, Lea & Blanchard had purchased advance proof sheets of volume three in London and seemed assured of an advantage over Harper & Bros., who had to wait for a published copy, which would then have to be set in type and printed. However, Harper & Bros. sent a fast vessel out to meet the inbound packet from England, obtained a copy of *Peveril of the Peak*, and returned to New York well ahead of the packet. Thus, they had a significant advantage over any other publishers in New York, but they still had to contend with Carey. Harper & Bros. rushed the book to its printing plant and, working nonstop, had it out to the booksellers within twenty-one hours, easily beating Carey, much to that firm's amazement and consternation. However, such victories did not come cheap, and soon Fletcher Harper and Henry Carey began to hammer out an agreement, which came to be known as the Harper Rule. It was agreed that any publisher who first announced his intention to reprint a British title would have exclusive claim to that title, and no other American publisher could reprint it (as had long been the custom known as "courtesy of the trade"). Even then, Harper usually printed such announcements in a New York paper and Carey in a Philadelphia paper, which naturally led to disagreements as to who had priority. In addition, publishers would print announcements concerning books they had not even had a chance to see, simply to get priority. Under the rule, publishers were required to purchase a proof copy from the British publisher as soon as it was available, though enforcement was very difficult. Even so, the Harper Rule was a good first step in sorting out the trade's internal problems. The next steps were much more difficult. The major problem remained of how a publisher might gain exclusive rights to an author. But the ultimate problem was how to enforce the rules across the trade, and this was never really resolved. Harper and Carey, having agreed on the easier aspects, disagreed intensely on the more difficult. With Carey's retirement in 1838, the crisis eased, but the problems remained.

The general business climate continued to deteriorate in the 1830s, culminating in the Panic of 1837. There had been a rapid increase in imports since 1832, and considerable sums of money had been sent out of the country to pay for these imports. The prices for many staples had more than doubled in only a few years. Flour, which had cost $5 per barrel in 1834, had shot up to $11 at the beginning of 1837; the price of corn had risen from $.53 per bushel to $1.15; and in February and March there had been bread riots in New York. With the demise of the Bank of the United States, the federal government had encouraged the formation of hundreds of new state banks with nominal capital, which flooded the country with paper money. Wild speculation occurred, especially in land, and millions of acres were bought on credit extended by these underfunded banks. When the banks began to call in their loans and to increase rates of interest, the Panic began. There was an epidemic of business failures, and more than a hundred banks collapsed. There was a universal suspension of payments, and credit evaporated.

The English novelist Captain Frederick Marryat visited New York at the time of the Panic and recorded his impressions in *A Diary in America.*

My appearance at New York was very much like bursting into a friend's house with a merry face when there is a death in it—with the sudden change from levity to condolence. Two hundred and sixty houses have already failed, and no one knows where it is to end. Suspicion, fear and misfortune have taken possession of the city. Not a smile on one countenance among the crowd who pass and repass; hurried steps, careworn faces, rapid exchanges of salutations, or hasty communication of anticipated ruin before the sun goes down. Here two or three are gathered together on one side, whispering and watching that they are not overheard; there a solitary, with his arms folded and his hat slouched, brooding over departed affluence. Mechanics, thrown out of employment, are pacing up and down with the air of famished wolves. The violent shock has been communicated like that of electricity, through the country to a distance of hundreds of miles. Canals, railroads, and all public works have been discontinued. … Every day fifteen or twenty merchants' names appear in the newspapers as bankrupts. … All the banks have stopped payment in specie, and there is not a dollar to be had. I walked down Wall Street, and had a convincing proof of the great demand for money, for somebody picked my pocket. The militia are under arms, as riots are expected. The banks in the country and other towns have followed the example of New York, and thus has General Jackson's currency bill been repealed without the aid of Congress. Affairs are now at their worst, and now that such is the case, the New Yorkers appear to recover their spirits. There certainly is a very remarkable energy in the American disposition; if they fall, they bound up again.

The availability of ready credit was a necessity for the publishing houses, whether large or small, and all were affected by the Panic. Many houses went under, but the House of Harper seemed untouched. The *Buffalo Literary Inquirer* noted: "These everlasting Harpers seem absolutely beyond the influence of all ordinary courses. The iron pressure that crushes the community has no perceptible effect on the presses of Cliff Street. Banks may stop—merchants break—commerce turn upside down—yet they still remain undaunted and unannoyed at their post, as caterers general to the literary world." In fact, even the House of Harper was hard pressed. When the Panic began, James was in Europe. The three other brothers were unable to agree among themselves on how to meet the crisis, and James was called home with great urgency. "The House of Harper shall not go to the wall," he stated resolutely upon his return, and the future of the firm was assured. But it was not without cost. New projects were deferred, the list was cut back, and the firm took on job printing. The Panic left the Harper brothers with a more conservative outlook and pushed them to adopt more stringent business practices, which no doubt solidified Harper & Bros.' position as the nation's premier publishing house, but at the same time it marked a shift away from an emphasis on literature and more to an emphasis on business.

In most instances, as previously mentioned, British authors received no royalties or compensation for the American editions of their works. And American authors were not much better off. The original concept of copyright in England, dating from the sixteenth century, was developed to protect the publisher, not the author. In 1710 Parliament passed a new copyright act that actually addressed the idea of an author's right to his or her intellectual property, much to the consternation of the book trade. The new act established the system of copyright that still pertains today, though with significant modification. The eighteenth-century book trade, in England and America, was not particularly inclined to change its habits in dealing with authors, but a series of lawsuits clearly established the rights of an author and the obligations of a publisher. Copyright was legally enforceable within the United States, but as the government had failed to agree to the international copyright convention, the works of British and other foreign authors were pirated with impunity.

Given the great popularity of many British authors and the huge number of their titles sold across the United States,

Though Charles Dickens was well received on his first American tour in 1842 and lionized as the greatest living English novelist, his tour was marred by his outspoken comments against slavery and his support of international copyright. Dickens became disillusioned with what he saw in America, and he voiced those disappointments in his letters to friends in England. "The Americans were admitted on all hands to have greatly refined upon the English language! I need not tell you that out of Boston and New York a nasal drawl is universal, but I may as well hint that the prevailing grammar is also more than doubtful; that the oddest vulgarisms are received idioms; ... and that the most fashionable and aristocratic (these are two words in great use), instead of asking you in what place you were born, inquire where you 'hail from'!"

authors such as Charles Dickens were losing out on a considerable income. For Dickens, who was always in need of income, this was an intolerable situation. In January 1842 the great author arrived in Boston, both to promote his novels and to force the issue of international copyright. Across the country his lectures were well attended and he was received with great acclaim, but his pleas on behalf of international copyright fell on deaf ears. American readers benefited from the piracies in being able to buy first-rate novels and other literature at rock-bottom prices. And though American readers might agree in principle that an author was due just compensation, they were unwilling to accept an increase in the price of books to provide that compensation. Dickens's tour was a triumphal progress, but on the question of copyright there was barely any progress at all.

It is hardly surprising that Harper and the other major publishers were little moved by Dickens's pleas, for as Parson Weems had pointed out to Matthew Carey some years before, the American reading public wants books, but they must be cheap books. Carey had climbed out of debt by pirating British authors and selling them in vast quantities at very cheap prices. Harper & Bros. had learned the same lesson, and in the very uncertain financial conditions of the 1830s and early 1840s the firm could not undertake an action that might lead it into bankruptcy. Harper & Bros. had been very active in developing new marketing techniques for its books as one way to ensure the firm's survival as the financial crisis deepened in the 1830s. Books

Any new work by Charles Dickens was guaranteed to be an instant bestseller, even one such as American Notes, *which portrayed America in an unfavorable light. American Notes was Dickens's response to his American tour in 1842, and it was published in 1842 in the midst of the "battle of the weeklies" in New York. The newspaperlike weeklies, such as* Brother Jonathan *illustrated here and the* New World, *published whole novels in a very cheap newspaper format that allowed them to take advantage of low postal rates for newspapers. The publishing houses were hard hit but fought back by issuing the same titles, in this instance Harper & Bros.'* American Notes, *in inexpensive book formats, taking a loss in the hope of driving the weeklies out of business. In fact, it was the U.S. Post Office that drove the weeklies out of the book business in 1843 by declaring these books to be ineligible for the low postal rates for newspapers.*

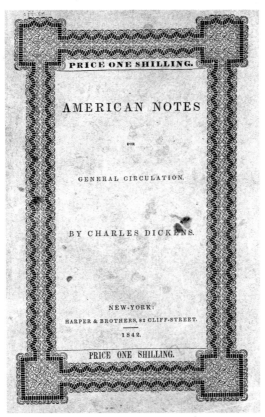

were not only sold by salesmen, but large quantities were also sold by mail through letters of solicitation and catalogues. The firm's books were to be found heading into the interior on canal boats and stagecoaches along the National Pike. In promoting their books, Harper & Bros. encouraged newspapers and magazines to publish at least simple notices of books, but even better to publish favorable reviews. These notices and reviews built sales and also built the reputation of Harper as the preeminent American publisher.

But not even the nation's preeminent publisher was immune to the continued economic slump after the Panic. In spite of better business practices, the efficient use of new technology, and effective marketing techniques, Harper faced its worst year yet in 1842. The firm's list consisted of only thirty-six titles, but profitability was maintained through vigorous sales of the "libraries" and textbooks. The greatest threat to Harper & Bros., and to all the other large houses, came in what has been called the Great Revolution in Publishing. The adoption of the new technologies—especially papermaking machines, cylinder presses, and stereotyped plates—had enabled publishers to produce well-made books at quite low costs, but it also meant that other publishers could produce poorly made books priced so low that they drove all other competitors out of the market. The publishing houses had been moving in this direction for several decades, but the mushrooming of cheap titles aimed at a mass market in the early 1840s, in conjunction with the economic slump, created great turmoil in the publishing world.

The crisis came to a dramatic head in the battle of the weeklies. The battle was between two New York weeklies, *Brother Jonathan* and the *New World*. These weeklies were supposedly magazines, but in fact they were vehicles for serialized novels, most often pirated British titles. Because they were produced like newspapers, they were very cheap, and even more important they were able to use the very low postal rate intended for newspapers. *Brother Jonathan* had been founded in 1839 by two New York journalists, Park Benjamin and Rufus Wilmot Griswold. After six months of great success they were fired by the new owner of their major backer. They acquired another partner and in June 1840 started the *New World*, a direct copy of *Brother Jonathan*. In July 1841 the two weeklies began to issue "supplements" and "extras," which contained whole novels printed in newspaper format. In the competition for readers, the weeklies pushed prices lower and lower. These newspaper novels were being sold on the street for fifty cents and even as low as twenty-five cents. In 1842, Bulwer's *Zanoni* was issued by both weeklies and by Harper at the same time, and was selling for as little as six cents a copy. Soon the newspaper publishers were bringing out their own supplements, and the book publishers found their stock of well-made novels priced at $1 to $2 a copy unsaleable. The rivalry was so intense that in June 1842 an employee of *Brother Jonathan* broke into Harper's bindery to steal a copy of a new novel that the firm had recently acquired in proofs from London. The thief then torched the building and destroyed the bindery. Harper & Bros. was able to rebuild, but it remained a prime target for such thievery. On Christmas Day of that year another thief broke in and this time stole Bulwer's *The Last of the Barons*. One response of the firm was to launch its own series of cheap novels, the reactivated Library of Select Novels, selling at twenty-five cents each. That price was soon cut in half, and other publishers cut prices even lower, to the point that no one was able to make a profit. The *New World* told its readers: "You are not so green as to pay a dollar for what you can get for eighteen pence or a shilling— not you! … We are friends of the people, and our motto is, 'The greatest good to the greatest number.'" The publishing houses met the low prices and glutted the market with cheap novels, but it was the United States Post Office that finally ended the crisis when in 1843 it ordered that the "supplements" had to be mailed as books and not at the much cheaper rate for newspapers. This effectively ended the crisis, as prices increased and readers grew increasingly dissatisfied with poorly made books and the newspaper format of the "supplements." Even so, inexpensive books produced for the mass market had become a permanent feature of American publishing.

Even the most impoverished reader could now afford to choose among the entire range of popular literature and other titles. Whatever the effect on the book trade, the crisis brought books into the homes and lives of many new readers and opened up whole new worlds for people who would become lifetime readers as a result, and who would pass the value of reading on to subsequent generations.

Brother Jonathan folded within seven months of the Post Office order, while the *New World* managed to continue until 1845. Out of the chaos of the crisis came a period of steady expansion, price stability, and profitability for the book trade. This was due in great part to the huge new readership that had been stimulated by the availability of affordable literature. Cheap books, in paper and hardbound, became a substantial part of almost every publisher's list, most selling for less than a dollar. Piracy was still important for some firms, but gradually American authors came to occupy a larger percentage of most publishers' lists. With such widespread prosperity, there was little need for price competition, and the idea of courtesy of the trade, which had been codified in the Harper Rule, became common.

During these prosperous years, Harper & Bros. had more than its share of successes. In 1843 the firm brought out an abridged version of Webster's *Dictionary*, which sold over 250,000 copies over the course of the next decade, at the end of which G.&C. Merriam obtained the plates and copyright. In 1844 *Harper's Illuminated and New Pictorial Bible* was published. Bibles had always been a standard part of most American publishers' lists and had often been very profitable. But this was no ordinary Bible. The illustrations were produced from woodcuts using the new technology of electrotyping. Like stereotype plates, electrotype plates are duplicates of the handset pages, which in this instance included woodcut illustrations in addition to type. A mold was made of the original type and illustrations and sprayed with a silver nitrate solution to make it electrically conductive. It was placed in an

Harper's Illuminated and New Pictorial Bible, *published in 1844, was a tour de force in the use of the new technology of electrotyping. The result has been called the finest book published in America up to that time. Harper & Bros. mounted a massive marketing campaign, selling the Bible in fifty-four serial parts in an edition of fifty thousand copies, and then in a regular edition of twenty-five thousand in 1846.*

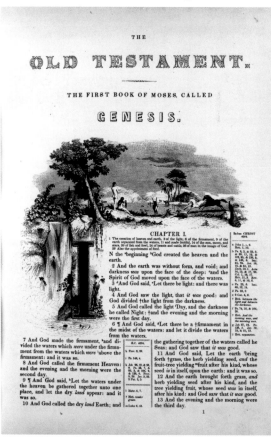

electroplating bath, where a thin shell of copper was deposited on it. The shell formed the surface of the new plate, which was backed with a layer of lead. The result was spectacular, and the Bible was perhaps the finest example of American book production to date. Harper & Bros. mounted a massive marketing campaign. The Bible could be purchased in serial parts, fifty-four parts of twenty-eight pages, priced at twenty-five cents each, thus making it affordable for even the most humble of households. The press run for this serial version was fifty thousand. A regular edition of twenty-five thousand was also issued in 1846, bound in elaborate gold-embossed morocco leather.

By the end of the decade, the firm had nineteen power presses turning out about two million volumes a year. Nearly 350 people worked in the firm's seven five-story buildings, and at the beginning of the new decade 1,549 books were in print, 722 original editions and 827 reprints. Harper & Bros. was not only the largest publisher in the United States, but the largest in the world. In June 1850, *Harper's New Monthly Magazine* was launched, and circulation climbed

On December 10, 1853, a fire started in the Harper plant that quickly engulfed the whole building. As it began at lunch time there were no fatalities, but the building was gutted. One bystander "professed to be able to tell when poetry went sparkling skyward, when romances cast a lurid glare around or when smoke as of Tophet came from the tomes of orthodox divinity."

After the disastrous fire of 1853, Harper & Bros. quickly rebuilt and opened two fireproof buildings on Franklin Square in 1855. For a time the new facility was a major tourist attraction.

The Narrative of the Life of Frederick Douglass *provides an eloquent and poignant account of what it was to be an African-American in antebellum America. Douglass had been born a slave in Maryland and secretly taught himself to read. He escaped via the Underground Railway in 1838 to New Bedford, Massachusetts. He first spoke in public about his experiences as a slave in 1841, and soon he became a full-time lecturer, and people were eager to read his story. His* Narrative *appeared in 1845 and was reprinted four more times within a year. Douglass's account was important for what it revealed about the inhumanity and bestiality of slavery, but Douglass himself was even more important because of his ability to convey to large numbers of people the image of a literate and articulate black man. This copy of the* Narrative *belonged to President Chester Arthur's father, who signed it in the upper right-hand corner.*

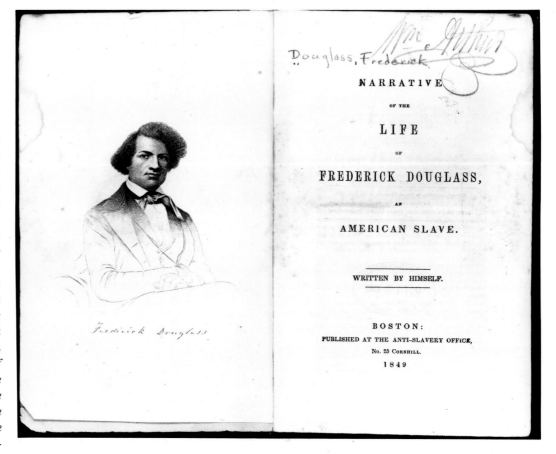

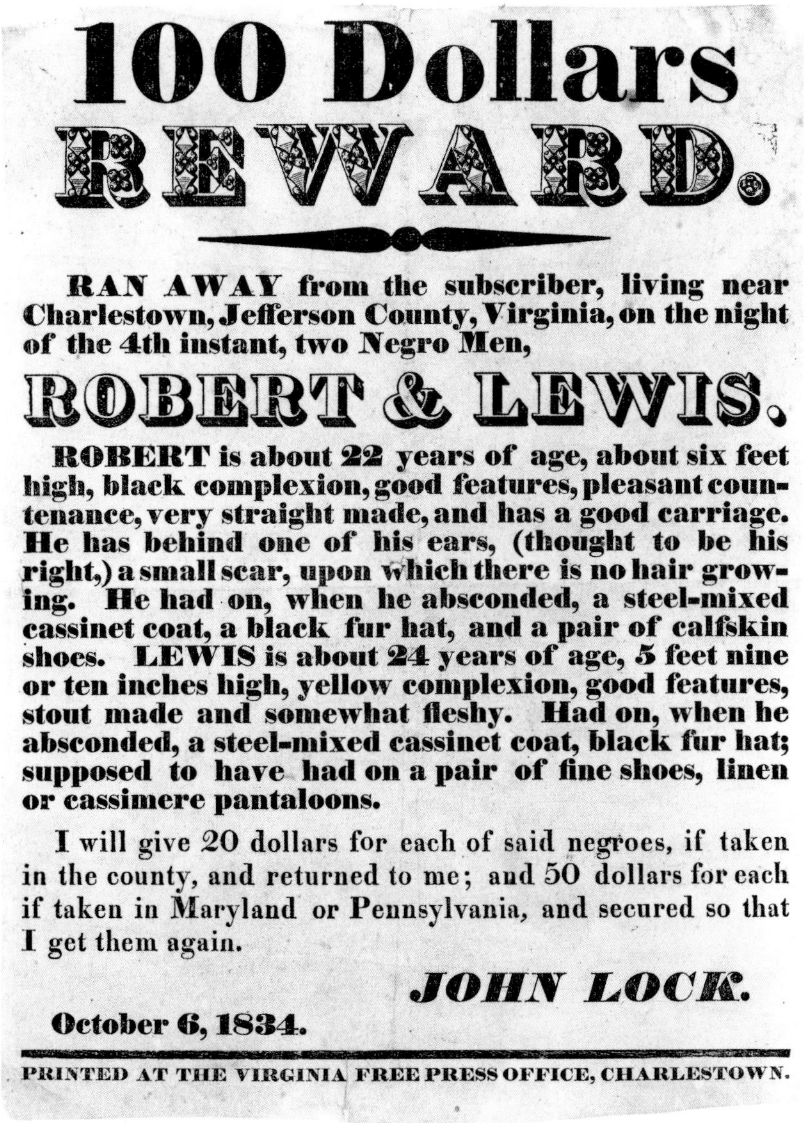

100 Dollars
REWARD.

RAN AWAY from the subscriber, living near Charlestown, Jefferson County, Virginia, on the night of the 4th instant, two Negro Men,

ROBERT & LEWIS.

ROBERT is about **22** years of age, about six feet high, black complexion, good features, pleasant countenance, very straight made, and has a good carriage. He has behind one of his ears, (thought to be his right,) a small scar, upon which there is no hair growing. He had on, when he absconded, a steel-mixed cassinet coat, a black fur hat, and a pair of calfskin shoes. **LEWIS** is about **24** years of age, **5** feet nine or ten inches high, yellow complexion, good features, stout made and somewhat fleshy. Had on, when he absconded, a steel-mixed cassinet coat, black fur hat; supposed to have had on a pair of fine shoes, linen or cassimere pantaloons.

I will give 20 dollars for each of said negroes, if taken in the county, and returned to me; and 50 dollars for each if taken in Maryland or Pennsylvania, and secured so that I get them again.

JOHN LOCK.

October 6, 1834.

PRINTED AT THE VIRGINIA FREE PRESS OFFICE, CHARLESTOWN.

This handbill offering a reward for escaped slaves illustrates the terror from which Douglass fled and under which his "brethren in bonds—faithfully relying upon the power of truth, love, and justice" continued to suffer. When Douglass published his Narrative, *he revealed his former owner's name and thus put his own freedom in jeopardy as an escaped slave. In order to remain free, he fled to England, where he lectured. Saving a sizable sum from his speaking engagements, he returned to America after about two years and purchased his freedom and established the newspaper* North Star.

Edgar Allan Poe, one of nineteenth-century America's most brilliant and imaginative writers, led a tortured and difficult life that was cut short in 1849 by heavy drinking. The son of itinerant actors, Poe was orphaned at an early age. He later attended both the University of Virginia and West Point but graduated from neither. His poetry began to appear in the late 1820s, and he found work as an editor, critic, and short-story writer for newspapers and magazines in Richmond, Philadelphia, and New York City. His essay "The Poetic Principle" is an intelligent critique that remains pertinent today. In 1838 he published The Narrative of Arthur Gordon Pym; *in 1840,* Tales of the Grotesque and Arabesque; *and in 1845,* The Raven and Other Poems, *which is illustrated here. Poe's fictive world is remarkable and compelling, particularly in such short stories as "The Fall of the House of Usher." His short story "The Murders in the Rue Morgue" is considered to be one of the earliest detective stories. Unlike other authors who were either unappreciated or unknown in their own time, Poe elicited strong responses. Emerson called him "the jingle man," and Lowell characterized him as "three-fifths genius and two-fifths sheer fudge." However, the great Irish poet W. B. Yeats said that he was "always and for all lands a great lyric poet."*

" *Sundry citizens of this good land, meaning well, and hoping well, prompted by a certain something in their nature, have trained themselves to do service in various Essays, Poems, Histories, and books of Art, Fancy, and Truth.*"

ADDRESS OF THE AMERICAN COPY-RIGHT CLUB.

WILEY AND PUTNAM'S

LIBRARY OF AMERICAN BOOKS.

NO. VIII.

THE RAVEN AND OTHER POEMS.

BY

EDGAR A. POE.

NEW YORK AND LONDON.

WILEY AND PUTNAM, 161 BROADWAY: 6 WATERLOO PLACE.

Price, Thirty-one Cents.

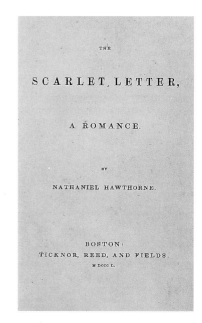

Nathaniel Hawthorne was born in Salem, Massachusetts, in 1804 to a prominent Puritan family. His father, a sea captain, died in 1808 and left his widow to a long life of mourning and seclusion, which no doubt influenced Hawthorne's own somber and melancholy outlook. After graduating from Bowdoin College in 1825, he returned to Salem to write, publishing in 1829 his first novel, Fanshawe, *an anonymous work that he financed himself and that went almost entirely unnoticed. In 1837 he found some success in a collection of short stories, the* Twice-Told Tales. *He lived for a time at Brook Farm, the transcendentalist experiment in communal living that included Emerson, Margaret Fuller, and Horace Greeley, among others, but his solitary ways were incompatible with the corporate life of the farm. His masterpiece, published in 1850, was* The Scarlet Letter, *and there soon followed* The House of the Seven Gables *and* The Blithedale Romance. *He went on to serve as American consul at Liverpool from 1853 to 1857 and then spent two years living in Italy. Out of his Italian experiences came his last novel,* The Marble Faun.

Hawthorne's fiction is highly symbolic, and in his masterpiece, The Scarlet Letter, *he explored the decadent moral and spiritual world of seventeenth-century Puritanism in his native Massachusetts. This romantic novel of guilt and conscience epitomizes the Puritan dilemma that fascinated and engaged Hawthorne for most of his life. It is a novel that continues to resonate and has become part of the American cultural fabric.*

Harriet Beecher Stowe, New Englander wife of a theology professor and mother of seven, first saw slavery in Kentucky in 1833 while living across the river in Cincinnati. She summed up her purpose in writing in a letter to the English novelist George Eliot, "Art as an end, not instrument, has little interest to me." She wrote a number of other works over the course of her long life, but none was as influential or as instrumental as Uncle Tom's Cabin, *which she wrote after moving to Maine in 1850. Photograph by N. Sarony, showing Stowe in her late sixties in about 1880.*

Uncle Tom's Cabin *was published at a time when the nation was undecided about the issue of slavery. In depicting slaves as humane and heroic and the system of slavery as inhumane and despicable, Stowe's book turned the tide of public opinion in the North against slavery. Originally serialized in the abolitionist weekly* National Era, *the novel was published in two volumes in Boston in 1852. The first printing of 5,000 copies sold out in two days, and within a year's time 300,000 copies had been sold, making* Uncle Tom's Cabin *the most popular American novel. It has remained continuously in print and has been translated into more than forty languages. It is said that during the Civil War, when President Lincoln met Stowe, he summed up the book's impact: "So you're the little woman who wrote the book that made this great war."*

UNCLE TOM'S CABIN;

OR,

LIFE AMONG THE LOWLY.

BY

HARRIET BEECHER STOWE.

VOL. I.

BOSTON:
JOHN P. JEWETT & COMPANY.
CLEVELAND, OHIO:
JEWETT, PROCTOR & WORTHINGTON.
1852.

Henry David Thoreau seemed to be the answer to Emerson's plea for an "American scholar." Thoreau considered himself "a mystic, a transcendentalist, and a natural philosopher to boot." But as towering a figure as he seems to us as we look back across the centuries, he was all but unknown in his lifetime. He made his living as a teacher, surveyor, lecturer, and handyman. Photograph by George F. Parlow.

WALDEN;

OR,

LIFE IN THE WOODS.

BY HENRY D. THOREAU,

AUTHOR OF "A WEEK ON THE CONCORD AND MERRIMACK RIVERS."

I do not propose to write an ode to dejection, but to brag as lustily as chanticleer in the
morning, standing on his roost, if only to wake my neighbors up. — Page 92.

Copy 2

BOSTON:
TICKNOR AND FIELDS.
M DCCC LIV.

Walden, *Thoreau's most famous book, recounts the time he spent living in a hut at Walden Pond from July 4, 1845, to September 6, 1847. Here in solitude he contemplated the natural cycles of life and lived "a life of simplicity, independence, magnanimity, and trust." Published in 1854, Walden had little immediate impact, but in time Thoreau's beliefs in the individual and in moral laws superior to the state have shaped American democracy and reinforced the American perspective in its unique emphasis on the rights of the individual.*

A map of Walden Pond, as surveyed by Thoreau in 1846 and included in the first edition of Walden.

When we look back across the literary scene of mid-nineteenth-century America, the figure of Herman Melville looms large. Even for many Americans who have never read Moby Dick, *the image of the obsessive pursuit of the great white whale is immediately recognizable and has become part of our national consciousness. But in his own time Melville was little appreciated, and he felt much discouragement: "Though I wrote the Gospels in this century, I should die in the gutter." Melville continued to produce important works but earned his living as a customs inspector in New York City. He died in poverty and obscurity, and his works were only rediscovered in this century. Frontispiece photograph from* Journal up the Straits, *Oct. 11, 1856–May 5, 1857 (New York: Colophon, 1935).*

Beadle's Dime Novels burst onto the scene in 1860. These cheaply produced sensational adventures and mystery tales were bound in bright paper covers that featured lurid woodcut illustrations and were designed to catch the reader's eye. At first priced at a dime, they soon were sold for a nickel, but the term "dime novel" stuck and came to describe the whole genre. Though the firm of Beadle & Co. suffered along with the whole book trade from wartime shortages, the dime novels proved extraordinarily popular, particularly among the soldiers in camp. By the end of the war, Beadle & Co. had sold over four million dime novels, but that was only the beginning. The dime novels concentrated on tales of the West and featured real-life heroes such as Buffalo Bill and Kit Carson and fictional ones such as Deadwood Dick and Rosebud Rob. The original orange covers were replaced in 1874 by multicolored covers that proved more competitive. Sales of dime novels declined at the end of the century, yet the imprint, Beadle's Dime Novels, continued until 1937.

steadily from 50,000 to 130,000 in 1853. In the early 1850s the Harper brothers could reasonably anticipate continued growth and prosperity as success built upon success, but on December 10, 1853, disaster struck. Somehow a fire started in a room containing camphine, a highly flammable liquid used to clean ink off the plates. Once started, there was no hope of putting it out. Luckily it started at 1 P.M., and most of the staff was at lunch, so there were no fatalities and few injuries. A huge crowd gathered to watch the futile efforts of the fire brigade. As reported in the press, one bystander "professed to be able to tell when poetry went sparkling skyward, when romances cast a lurid glare around or when smoke as of Tophet came from the tomes of orthodox divinity." Almost nothing was saved, and the whole plant was a loss, estimated at more than $1 million. The firm was self-insured, which meant the Harpers had to absorb the loss and finance the new building. Had such a catastrophe occurred in the 1830s the firm might well have gone under, but having more than a decade of extraordinary prosperity behind it, the firm was able to build a new plant in two fireproof buildings on Franklin Square, which opened in the summer of 1855.

Recovery was quick for Harper & Bros., which soon regained its position as the world's largest publisher. This was a boom time for the nation. The discovery of gold in California, the rapid expansion of rail lines, and the establishment of steamships regularly crossing the seas had propelled the economy to new heights of prosperity, but at the same time many firms were overextended, and speculation in many questionable ventures continued at a pace that could not be maintained. The limit was reached in 1857 when the growth of the economy slowed, credit contracted, and firms began to fail. The Panic of 1857 brought down a number of publishing houses, and even Harper & Bros. again had a difficult time. In October the firm was transferred into the hands of two members of the next generation, John W. and Joseph W. Harper, to protect it from the demands creditors were making on the founding brothers. Such extreme measures were often necessary as the American economy cycled through exaggerated periods of boom and bust.

At the end of the decade a new phenomenon burst onto the scene:

BOOKS FOR THE MILLION!
A Dollar Book for a Dime!!
128 pages complete, only Ten Cents!!

BEADLE'S DIME NOVELS NO. 1
MALAESKA:
Indian Wife of the White Hunter
by Mrs. Ann S. Stephens
128 pages, 12 mo. Ready Saturday Morning, June 9

The series, Beadle's Dime Novels, first appeared in 1860, the creation of Robert Adams and Irwin and Erastus Beadle, who published as Irwin P. Beadle & Co. in New York.

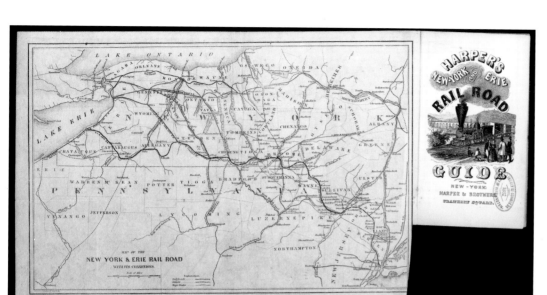

The new railroads had a large impact on both readers and the book trade. Whereas previously publishers and distributors had to rely on water-borne transport or nearly nonexistent roads to get books to readers in the interior, the development of the railroads made distribution far easier and made the development of regional centers such as Chicago possible. In addition, some publishers saw an opportunity in the "captive audience" of railroad passengers. Following the example of British firms such as W.H. Smith, American publishers targeted railroad readers with inexpensive titles of adventure and romance, often in colorful covers with eye-catching illustrations. These titles, sold at railway stations, were designed to provide light reading for rail journeys and proved very popular. On a more practical level, Harper published the railroad guide shown here in 1854.

The firm had issued a number of successful volumes, such as *Beadle's Dime Song Book* in 1859, followed by the *Dime Cook Book*, *Dime Recipe Book*, *Dime Dialogues*, *Dime Speaker*, and the *Dime Methodist*. Though the first "dime novel" actually sold for a dime, most sold for a nickel; even so, the term "dime novel" persisted and came to describe a particular kind of literature. Typically, the dime novel was a sensational adventure or mystery tale. It was bound in a yellow or orange paper cover that included a lurid woodcut illustration on the front. It was designed to catch the eye and was priced for even the most modest income. The dime novels were an instant success, but with the advent of the Civil War, fewer books could be printed due to wartime shortages and restrictions. On the other hand, the kind of fiction published in the dime novels was exactly what the troops wanted to read, and great numbers of dime novels found their way into army camps. The troops were hungry for almost any reading material, but preferred dime novels over other kinds. After the war, a popular magazine noted that "the Dime Novels became not only household words in all sections of the country, but were the soldier's solace and comfort … and contributed, in a wonderful degree, to ameliorate the trials and suffering of army life." As the war ended, there were hundreds of thousands of veterans who would buy each new dime novel as fast as Beadle & Co. could produce them. By the middle of 1865, the firm had published over four million dime novels, but this was just the beginning, as Beadle & Co., and indeed the whole book trade, entered a new era of prosperity.

Abraham Lincoln reading to his son, "Tad." Photograph by Anthony Berger in Mathew B. Brady's Gallery, Washington, D.C., February 9, 1864.

Two small girls reading. Photoprint frontispiece from Henry Peach Robinson's Pictorial Effect in Photography, 1869.

Reading in America

Reading has always been an integral part of the American experience. Books arrived with the first colonists and continue to find a place in virtually every American household. Even those who are illiterate recognize the power and necessity of reading. For many, reading has been the means to education and success. In the early years of our nation books were often the only connection to the wider cultures of learning and civilization. Many, like Abraham Lincoln, taught themselves through reading without the benefit of formal education. For many others, reading has opened windows onto many different worlds that have provided color, excitement, and pleasure for millions of Americans of all ages in all walks of life. And while reading has enriched individual citizens beyond measure, it has created much more in an educated and literate citizenry that ensures the continuance of American democracy. In colonial America readers tended to concentrate on a few important books, such as the Bible, and read and re-read them, but with the proliferation of books and periodicals in the nineteenth century, people began to read widely and extensively, though perhaps without the intensity of their forebears. With the development of serialized books, readers consumed titles in intense, short, monthly spurts, divided by longer periods in which the text could be contemplated. But however one reads a book, there develops an intimate relationship between author and reader. One recent study, *Books That Made the Difference* by Gordon and Patricia Sabine, demonstrated how vital the act of reading is. "What we learned from listening to America was that *all* reading is good, that *no one* else can predict what will make the greatest difference in any individual's life. Censors presume to know what difference a book will make to certain individuals, and this is the great flaw in their approach, for after this study, we *know* that this is an unrealistic presumption. No censor can foretell what will motivate the bored, inform the unknowing, inspire even the genius."

Couple reading at home in Boston. Photograph by Charles H. Currier, ca. 1895.

Immediate right: Boy reading on a bench, Washington, D.C., ca. 1920.

Far right: Child of a sharecropper reading on the bed in the living room of their cabin, New Madrid, Missouri. Photograph by Russell Lee for the Farm Security Administration, May 1938.

Sharecropper reading in his living room, New Madrid, Missouri. Photograph by Russell Lee for the Farm Security Administration, May 1938.

Buckboard Charlie reading the American Legion Monthly *in the living room of his shack, Iron River, Michigan. Photograph by Russell Lee for the Farm Security Administration, April 1937.*

Sunday afternoon on the front porch, Vincennes, Indiana. Photograph by John Vachon for the Farm Security Administration, July 1941.

Books have always been special for children, particularly for young girls who dream of owning a pony. This poster was created by the Center for the Book in the Library of Congress to celebrate the Year of the Young Reader in 1989. It was adapted from a photograph by William Kuntzman, "The Magic of Reading."

IV
Industrialization and Expansion
1865–1918

ith the Civil War behind it, the nation resumed its course of expansion, both geographic and economic. The railroads now spanned the continent, and the industrial base that had propelled the North to victory was now poised to transform an agrarian nation into an industrial powerhouse. It was seen as a future full of endless opportunities that would bring boundless prosperity to all. One merely had to look to the past to see the exhilarating and inexorable movement of American progress. Horace Greeley's often repeated advice, "Go west, young man," epitomized the nation's spirit as Americans marched toward a better life, both in the West and in the newly industrialized cities.

The creation of a national economy, knit together by the railroads, in turn created a national culture and a national reading public. In the past, when books and other reading materials were scarce and expensive, readers had tended to concentrate on a few books, such as the Bible or Bunyan's *Pilgrim's Progress*, and intensively read and re-read them. But now with the proliferation of inexpensive books and periodicals, people were able to read a wide variety of titles, though, ironically, vast numbers of readers tended to read the same things, as one bestseller followed another. This commonality of reading, however, created a shared context among millions of diverse people that further shaped and strengthened our national culture. During these years following the Civil War, the publishing industry developed a close and intimate relationship with the reading public and reflected (and formed) American national culture to a degree unparalleled until the advent of television in the second half of the twentieth century. During this period the nation developed a mature national literature that could rival that of any of the old countries. In short, the United States finally cut most of its dependent ties to Europe, both economically and intellectually, and it could be truthfully asserted that America had come of age.

Intimately connected with the expansion of literacy, fostered in part by the widespread establishment of public schools, was the development of public libraries across the nation. The first library supported by municipal taxes specifically for libraries was the Boston Public Library, established in 1854. By 1875 there were 257 public libraries, a number that was soon to increase dramatically. A major impetus for the establishment of new public libraries was the industrialist Andrew Carnegie, who between 1881 and 1920 donated $50 million toward building public libraries in towns and cities across the nation. By 1923 almost a third of the population was served by a Carnegie library, and by 1926 more than half of the population had access to a local library. Even those Americans too poor to purchase books now had free access to them through the local public library.

After the Civil War the great publishing houses continued to flourish, but now under the sons of the founders. These old-line firms were characterized by a conservatism that derived from their familial nature as father was succeeded by son, who was succeeded by grandson, and so forth. This was both a strength and a weakness, as the great houses showed enormous staying power but at the same time lacked flexibility. The old guard resisted the rise of advertising, the increased status of authors, and, even worse, the increased role of their agents. They resisted the increasing popular demand for entertainment and the trend to view books as merchandise. In the end, however, these historical trends could not be denied, and the great houses and the newcomers alike either adapted or failed.

The first of the new generation after the Civil War was Henry Holt, who in 1866 began a partnership with Frederick Leypoldt. In the same year, Patrick John Kenedy succeeded his father, as did Frank H. Dodd a year later. In 1869 George Brett established the New York office of Macmillan, Fleming H. Revell began publishing in Chicago, and Cornell University established its own press. In 1870 Frank H. Dodd joined with E. S. Mead to form Dodd, Mead & Co., and in 1872 George Haven Putnam took over the firm upon his father's sudden death. A year later Henry Holt became sole owner of his firm, and in 1875 P. F. Collier set up business. In 1876 Thomas Y. Crowell started publishing, as did Isaac K. Funk, who was joined by A. W. Wagnalls two years later. Johns Hopkins University Press was established in 1878, and in Boston the firm of Houghton, Osgood & Co. was formed. In 1879 Charles Scribner, Jr., assumed control of the firm his father had founded. The following year George Harrison Mifflin joined Houghton in Boston. In 1882 David McKay began publishing in Philadelphia, and in the next year the firms of A. L. Burt & Co. and Frederick A. Stokes & Co. were founded. The year 1884 saw John Macrae join E. P. Dutton, and the founding of Mark Twain's publishing venture, Charles L. Webster & Co., in Hartford. In 1885 Silver, Burdett & Co. began in Boston, and in Philadelphia Lippincott became the first firm to incorporate, at a capital of a million dollars.

A row of Adams bed-and-platen presses in Harper's new building, 1855. Harper & Bros. operated thirty Adams presses, most of which were tended by women.

The pace continued as W.B. Saunders was founded in Philadelphia in 1888, the American Book Co. in 1890 as the result of a large merger of several textbook houses, the University of Chicago Press in 1892, the University of California Press and Columbia University Press in 1893, Scott, Foresman & Co. in Chicago in 1896, Doubleday, McClure & Co. in 1897. In the same year D. Appleton & Co. incorporated at $2 million in capital. In 1899 Grosset & Dunlap began business, Harper & Bros. declared bankruptcy but reorganized and carried on, and McGraw Publishing Co. was established. Scribner was incorporated with $2 million in capital in 1903, and in the same year Princeton University Press, the World Book Co., and World Publishing Co. were established. Western Publishing was established in a small shop in Racine, Wisconsin, in 1907, and the next year saw the foundation of the Yale University Press. In 1913 the Harvard University Press was established, as was Prentice-Hall. During the First World War years the firm of Alfred A. Knopf was founded, New York University Press was established, and Boni & Liveright launched the Modern Library series.

The latter half of the nineteenth century saw an acceleration in technological developments in the book trade that led to the eventual mechanization of virtually every aspect of physical book production. Power-driven printing presses had become common early in the century, especially the mammoth cylinder presses used by the large newspapers. The cylinder press was ideal for newspapers, for which speed was the overriding concern and quality mattered little. Books required the use of a platen press, which had developed in the first part of the century into a mechanical version of the original platen press invented by Gutenberg. In the 1830s Isaac and Seth Adams of Boston developed one of the first successful bed-and-platen presses, which was a significant improvement over the original platen press, and it was soon converted to use with steam power. Adams presses were soon adopted across the industry, and when Adams's greatest competitor, the preeminent American press manufacturer R. Hoe & Co., bought out the firm in 1859, the Adams press was continued and improved with new vigor. The Adams press enabled American printers to produce first-class work at speeds of between five hundred to one thousand impressions an hour. Such presses were used well into the twentieth century, but by the 1870s new cylinder and rotary presses were overtaking them. These presses had overcome the shortcomings of their earlier versions and were capable of fast, high-quality printing on both sides of the sheet and in more than one color. By the end of the century these presses were wholly automated, and the pressman had been transformed into a machine operator.

Similarly, the compositor who had set each piece of type by hand at the beginning of the century was transformed into a keyboard operator at the close of the century. Numerous attempts had been made to mechanize the process of composition, but most inventors worked with machines that would compose and distribute precast type. In 1885 Ottmar Mergenthaler rejected the use of precast type and developed a hot-metal composition machine that produced newly cast type in solid lines of metal. This device was soon known as the Linotype machine. In 1886 the first Linotype was installed at the *New York Tribune*, where it was very successful. Soon Linotype machines became standard equipment for newspapers across the country. Linotype machines were also adopted for book production (in contrast to the British adoption of the Monotype hot-metal process that set single newly cast pieces of type rather than a solid line). The compositor no longer filled his composing stick one piece of type at a time but now sat before a keyboard and pressed keys at a far faster rate.

The nineteenth century also saw the transformation of the binding trade from craft to mechanized industry. In turn, each of the bookbinding processes came to be mechanized. The rolling press was introduced in 1823 to press the folded sections or gatherings of the book. Next a machine was developed to prepare the covering cloth, at first a simple rolling press that applied dried starch to the cloth, resulting in an even-colored surface; from the 1830s on it had the capacity to do embossing and give the cloth a relief pattern. In 1832 an embossing press was developed that could apply gilded or blind-stamped titles and the like. Steam-powered folding machines were developed in the 1860s and 1870s, and during the same period several sewing machines were also introduced. These were followed by rounding and backing machines in the 1880s, case-making machines in the 1890s, and gathering machines in the first years of the 1900s. Finally, in 1903 a casing-in machine was created that combined all the binding processes in one machine.

By the beginning of the twentieth century, the whole process of making the physical book had been transformed, though the book itself was little changed in outward appearance. The publishing industry had also undergone changes, but nothing as radical as in the press rooms and binderies. The publishing houses were developing specialized positions and departments. Publishers were no longer able to read every manuscript that came in, and by the end of the century editorial assistants were making decisions on manuscripts. Readers were hired to evaluate manuscripts and were typically paid $5 for each report. Publishers and editors were becoming more assertive in their relations with authors, and rather than waiting for a completed manuscript, publishers worked with authors to develop book ideas. But authors, who had traditionally been treated with little consideration, came to rely on literary agents to represent them, much to the publishers' amazement and disgust. An agent was able to negotiate better financial terms and obtain more control over how a book was edited and designed. Henry Holt spoke for his fellow publishers when he said, "Royalties exceeding 10 percent are immoral." Holt rarely gave his authors written contracts, and as late as 1910 one of his authors had to ask for a contract for a book already in the press. In the past, most new or unknown authors had been required to pay for the costs of the printing plates and even provide an outright subsidy. Typically, publishers withheld royalties until about one thousand copies of a book had been sold and then paid 10 percent of the retail price, though prominent authors might get 20 percent. Advances appeared at about the turn of the century and came to replace the outright purchase of an author's manuscript.

Publishers often complained about how little profit there was in the trade. And certainly if one took an average book and looked at the accounting ledger, this was true. For example, William Lee, of Lee & Shepard, wrote in 1885:

A book of four hundred pages is considered an edition at 1000, and the total cost, including advertising, copyright, books to the press for review, and all incidentals is about $1250. This first edition, if all sold, will bring a

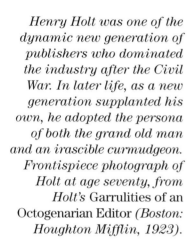

Henry Holt was one of the dynamic new generation of publishers who dominated the industry after the Civil War. In later life, as a new generation supplanted his own, he adopted the persona of both the grand old man and an irascible curmudgeon. Frontispiece photograph of Holt at age seventy, from Holt's Garrulities of an Octogenarian Editor *(Boston: Houghton Mifflin, 1923).*

net return of only $675, leaving $550 unaccounted for. A second edition will cost only $450, as the plates are on hand, and there is no expense on that score; and on that edition the return will again be $675, leaving still $225 of the original expenditure to be gotten out of the work. On the next edition, if it can be disposed of, this shortage is cleared up and a very small profit remains. So it can be seen that to be a slightly profitable investment, there must be at least three editions of 1000 copies of every book published. How can publishers be blamed for their extreme caution?

Yet this account leaves out all consideration of the bestseller, which could be extraordinarily profitable, or the steady seller from the backlist, both of which have always subsidized the more mundane and less profitable books on a publisher's list.

Publishing has always been an odd kind of business, in which the act of creating an intellectual object, a book, has been far more important than the traditional concerns of business. This distinction was summarized in the first issue of the *American Publishers' Circular and Literary Gazette* in 1863:

> The publisher's calling is not, in truth, a mere trade. He is the dispenser of knowledge to the community, and even his material interests are best served by whatever excites and appeals unto that desire for knowledge which is his lofty mission to satisfy.

While some might find this somewhat exaggerated and simplistic, it nonetheless expresses that unique quality that has attracted some of the nation's most talented people to a business that has had little to recommend it from a strictly business perspective. In 1905 Walter Hines Page echoed this point when he wrote that "publishing, as publishing, is the least profitable of all the professions, except preaching and teaching, to each of which it is a sort of cousin." But counterpoised to this gloomy assessment he continued, "A good book is a Big Thing, a thing to be thankful

Mark Twain was as different from Hawthorne, Emerson, and Thoreau as the West was from the East. Twain exemplified the optimistic, outward-looking, adventurous spirit of the American frontier, in contrast to the backward-looking, introspective somberness of those who had inherited Massachusetts Puritanism. Though literary critics have often judged Twain's work to be uneven and inferior to that of Hawthorne or Melville, the American public quickly embraced Twain as a great literary figure and as one who embodied the essence of the American spirit. Twain, who was born Samuel Clemens, left school at an early age to be apprenticed to a printer, and he subsequently worked as a journeyman printer in the early 1850s. In the years before the Civil War he worked as a steamboat pilot on the Mississippi, and with the outbreak of war, he briefly joined a group of Confederate volunteers. In 1862 he became a journalist in Nevada and embarked on a literary career. By 1865 he had established a reputation that continued to grow over the years. In 1870 he married and left the West for Hartford, Connecticut. There he became a partner in a publishing firm that published his books and made huge profits on Ulysses S. Grant's Memoirs. In time the firm ran into trouble with unprofitable books and large investments in mechanized typesetting equipment that never worked. As a result Twain was forced to declare bankruptcy in 1894. Over the course of the next four years he toured and lectured and wrote a number of uneven works, such as Tom Sawyer, Detective, *that brought in substantial income and allowed him to pay off his debts. Twain never regained the optimistic vigor and humor of his earlier works, and a strain of pessimism dominated his final years. Here Twain is pictured at Quarry Farm in Elmira, N.Y., with one of his tenant farmers, John Lewis.*

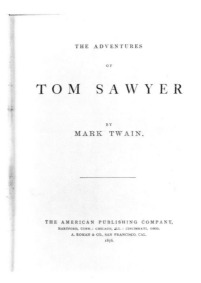

THE ADVENTURES

OF

TOM SAWYER

BY

MARK TWAIN.

THE AMERICAN PUBLISHING COMPANY,
HARTFORD, CONN.; CHICAGO, ILL.; CINCINNATI, OHIO.
A. ROMAN & CO., SAN FRANCISCO, CAL.
1876.

Tom Sawyer *(1876), followed by* Life on the Mississippi *(1883) and* Huckleberry Finn *(1884), represents the zenith of Twain's writings. This picaresque adventure novel celebrates the vitality and vigor of life on the Mississippi and in the newly settled regions in the middle of the country. In these works of Mark Twain the frontier spirit found a voice that still resonates today.*

Horatio Alger, Jr., was the product of a strict Puritan upbringing. After graduating from Harvard Divinity School, he rejected his background and lived the Bohemian life in Paris for a time. Returning to Massachusetts, he served as a Unitarian minister, but in 1866 he moved to New York and embarked on a literary career. He wrote nearly 130 books for boys, all of which are variants on the theme of a poor boy who struggles against temptation to win out by becoming rich and famous. These very popular books were the embodiment of the "American dream" and influenced countless boys to strive for success. Typical of these titles was Do and Dare, *illustrated here in an edition from 1905, though it first appeared in 1884. Alger's* Ragged Dick *series, begun in 1867, was his most popular. But* Tattered Tom, *begun in 1871, was also wildly successful. Altogether, more than twenty million copies of Alger's novels were published.*

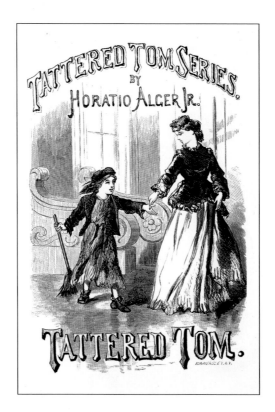

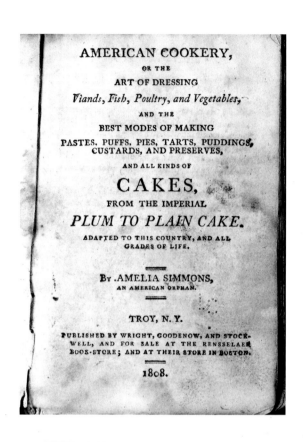

The first American cookbook was Amelia Simmons's American Cookery. *Published in Hartford in 1796, this modest work of forty-eight pages sold for only two shillings and three pence. Although English cookbooks had long been available to Americans, Simmons's book was the first to deal with the peculiarities of American foods such as corn, tomatoes, and potatoes and the often primitive conditions of the American kitchen.*

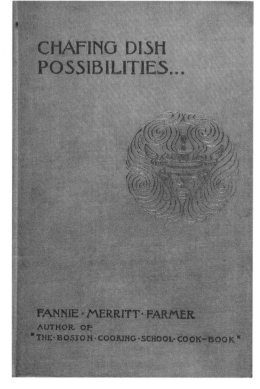

The Boston Cooking School opened in 1879 and had a profound influence on American etiquette and cookery. In 1884 Mary Lincoln wrote the Boston Cook Book, *but it was the publication of Fannie Farmer's* Boston Cooking-School Book *in 1896 that set the standard for all subsequent American cookbooks. Farmer was known as the "Mother of Level Measurements," and her books helped raise American cookery standards to the level of the European cuisines.*

Like Mark Twain, Walt Whitman started out as a printer and then a journalist, editing and writing for at least ten papers in New York and Brooklyn. In 1848 he traveled to New Orleans, where he worked for a time, and then back to New York by way of St. Louis and Chicago. At about this time Whitman went through a transformation that continues to be the subject of critical controversy. Whatever the root of his transformation, he now saw the world with new eyes. He reveled in the pleasures and pastimes of common people and celebrated himself as an average man. With a new vision he became extraordinarily sensitive to the varieties of life that swirled around him and combined to make up America. In 1855 he published twelve poems under the title Leaves of Grass. At first the book went almost entirely unnoticed, but Whitman continued to revise it. He found a trade publisher for the third edition in 1860 and with that enlarged edition began to achieve recognition. He spent much of the Civil War in Washington tending the wounded in army hospitals, and he felt the loss of Lincoln deeply, as he expressed in his dirges, "When Lilacs Last in the Dooryard Bloom'd" and "O Captain! My Captain!" He continued to issue new editions of the Leaves, in 1867 and 1871, but in 1873 he suffered a paralytic stroke. He spent his last nineteen years in Camden, New Jersey, where in spite of his condition he continued to write and revise Leaves of Grass.

Walt Whitman was greatly affected by the assassination of Abraham Lincoln, and he wrote two dirges on the occasion, one of which, "O Captain! My Captain!" is illustrated here in the poet's own hand. It was published in Sequel to Drum-Taps (1865–1866) and in Leaves of Grass (1867).

Owen Wister, grandson of the actress Fanny Kemble, made a number of trips from his native Pennsylvania to the wilds of Wyoming in the 1890s. His experiences among the cowboys provided material for several stories, but it was his novel, The Virginian, *set in Wyoming in the 1870s and 1880s, that brought him popular acclaim. In* The Virginian *he coined the memorable phrase, "When you call me that, smile!"*

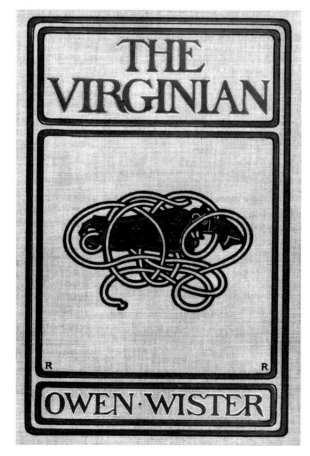

The Virginian: The Horseman of the Plains, *published in 1902, was a bestseller whose hero remained nameless, known only as "the Virginian." The popularity of this romantic vision of life among the cattle barons did much to shape the later generations' view of the American frontier, one that has been perpetuated in western novels, movies, and television programs.*

L. Frank Baum, originally a journalist, captured the nation's fancy in 1900 when he wrote The Wonderful Wizard of Oz. *He adapted it as a musical spectacular,* The Wizard of Oz, *in 1901 and went on to pen another thirteen books about Oz.*

Even after Baum's death in 1919, different authors continued the Oz series. Through these books, read by countless children and adults, and together with the musical film The Wizard of Oz, *released in 1939, Baum's fantasy world has become a permanent part of American culture.*

to heaven for. It is a great day for any of us when we can put our imprint on it. Here is a chance for reverence, for something like consecration." His fellow publishers invested every year "in books and authors that they know cannot yield a direct or immediate profit, and they make these investments because they feel ennobled by trying to do a service to literature."

Of the new generation after the Civil War, Henry Holt was one of the most prominent and influential men on the New York publishing scene. He was born in Baltimore in 1840 and began at Yale in 1861. Though trained in the law, he began to dabble in publishing with a fellow classmate, George Palmer Putnam. In about 1864 he met a German immigrant, Frederick Leypoldt, who ran a small publishing firm that specialized in translating German works. The two men liked each other right away and in 1866 formed a partnership, Leypoldt & Holt. Holt brought $11,000 to the partnership and was appalled to learn that Leypoldt's financial contribution was a debt of $11,000. Still, Leypoldt brought his talent and experience, and Holt learned a great deal from him. The firm specialized in foreign-language textbooks and translations that proved quite profitable. In time, Leypoldt departed to devote himself to the *Literary Bulletin and Trade Circular,* which would soon become

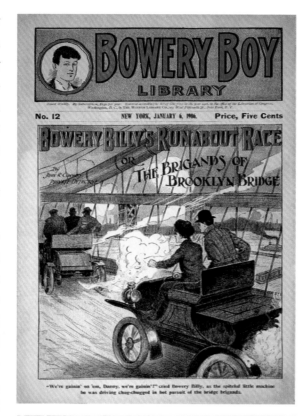

The Bowery in New York City gained its name because it once ran through Peter Stuyvesant's farm, or bouwerie. *In the nineteenth century it was notorious as a rough area known for its criminal haunts, drinking establishments, and dance halls. The Bowery boy was a stock figure who first appeared in the play* A Glance at New York *in 1848. He was an impudent rascal dressed in red shirt, turned-up trousers, and a plug hat.*

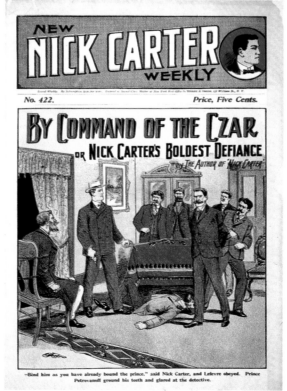

Nick Carter was the dime-novel hero of over one thousand titles. He first appeared in the works of John Russell Coryell in the 1880s, but many authors, including Frederick Dey, wrote Nick Carter books. Indeed, many authors adopted the name Nick Carter as a pseudonym, and anything having to do with Nick Carter was immensely popular. The books, stories, and magazines continued to flourish well into the twentieth century.

Edith Wharton was born in New York of a distinguished family in 1862. Educated privately, she first published a collection of short stories in 1899. She wrote that "every great novel must first of all be based on a profound sense of moral values, and then constructed with a classical unity and economy of means." The author must "bear in mind at each step that his business is not to ask what the situation would be likely to make of his characters, but what his characters, being what they are, would make of the situation." Wharton was a prolific author, but it was with the publication of The House of Mirth *in 1905 that she first achieved wide renown. Drawing on her background in New York, she wrote of false values and mores in the world of New York high society. Her finest novel is considered to be* The Age of Innocence, *which was published in 1920 and brought her the Pulitzer Prize, the first awarded to a woman.*

Publishers Weekly. Holt had a junior partner for a time, but in 1873 the firm became simply Henry Holt & Co.

Holt had become one of the nation's leading publishers by 1880. His list contained over three hundred titles, about which he noted, "one-fifth paid a large profit, one-fifth never paid for printing, and the rest barely paid their own expenses." One of his innovations was a series called the Condensed Classics, which anticipated this popular form in the twentieth century. Holt described their purpose as to remove "everything that a skillful novel reader would skip, and everything he might skip if he knew what was coming." He also created the American Science Series and the Leisure Hour Series, which was described as "a collection of works whose character is light and entertaining, though not trivial. While they are handy for the pocket or satchel, they are not, either in contents or appearance, unworthy of a place on the library shelves."

Many publishers and editors were known for their ability to pick a bestseller from the many, many manuscripts that passed through their offices each year, but as many successes as a publisher might have, there were the legendary tales of opportunities missed. It was not always apparent that a particular manuscript would be popular. A case in point is Anthony Hope's *The Prisoner of Zenda.* Late in 1893 Hope took his

Lew Wallace enjoyed writing in the open air in the yard of his Indiana home. A distinguished general who had saved Washington, D.C., from capture during the Civil War, Wallace wrote one of the greatest bestsellers of all time, Ben Hur. *Published in 1880, it has sold over two million copies and has been translated into many foreign languages.*

manuscript to E.P. Dutton, where John Macrae, president of the firm, declined to publish it. Macrae suggested he take it to Henry Holt, who published it the following year. It was an instant bestseller that remained in print for many years. Just before Christmas 1895, Holt visited Macrae and gave him a handsome gold tie clasp as a token of his gratitude for sending Hope and *The Prisoner of Zenda* to him. Macrae greatly cherished the tie clasp and wore it nearly every day. One of his editors recounted that at meetings when editors were arguing over the rejection of a manuscript that Macrae favored, the old man would tap his tie clasp so that his editors might profit from his rejection of *The Prisoner of Zenda*. But Holt too had his share of missed opportunities. He rejected Joseph Conrad because his earlier books had poor sales and Lincoln Steffens because he believed people did not want to read about poor people and slums.

Holt began a gradual retirement in 1910 at the age of seventy. He announced to his staff that they would have to learn to get along without him, as he was no longer coming in. Many of his staff no doubt wished that he would stay away, but that was impossible. In spite of his retirement he remained *de facto* head of the firm, and no decisions were made without him. However, in that same year, he promoted Alfred Harcourt, who had joined the firm in 1904, to head the trade department. Harcourt proved to be an exceptional editor, and as Holt gradually retired, Harcourt easily filled his place, at least as publisher. No one, however, could ever truly replace the irascible Henry Holt, who announced to the trade that he was not "impressed that the horizon is in any way crowded by worthy successors to the publishers of a generation ago."

As Holt looked back over the last half century, he certainly must have seen at least one worthy successor in Frank N. Doubleday, who as Christopher Morley noted, was "really the first of a new era in book publishing—which he visualized foremost as a business, not merely as a dignified literary avocation." Doubleday, born in 1862, began in the trade at an early age. At fourteen he had to leave school and find full-time work. Wanting to enter the publishing business, he considered which of the New York houses was the best and settled on Scribner. He tells the story in his own words:

> So I worked up a letter of introduction from A.S. Barnes & Co., educational publishers, to Mr. J. Blair Scribner, which I presented and asked if he did not want to hire a boy. He said he did not—that he did not hire boys—anyhow that was Mr. Armstrong's business.
>
> So I tackled Mr. Armstrong, whose desk was next to Mr. Scribner's and asked him if he did not want to hire a boy. He said he did not need any.

Frank N. Doubleday and his wife on board their launch at their winter home, Jungle Cove, Nassau, 1930. If Henry Holt was the backward-gazing, old curmudgeon, Frank Doubleday was the optimistic, forward-looking publisher of the future.

"This is the fifteenth of December," I argued, "and you will need help over Christmas. I think you had better take me. It will cost you only three dollars a week."

He still resisted my blandishments and insisted that he did not need me, but I told him: "You will make a great mistake if you don't take me on. If you hire me, you will get a good boy."

"You seem to have a high opinion of yourself," he remarked.

"Yes," I replied, "I have. I only ask the chance to see if I can't get you to think as favorably of me as I do of myself."

"Well," said he, "you are so cheeky that I'll give you a job for a week."

I was there eighteen years.

Doubleday proved to be even better than his self-recommendation promised. He worked his way up from carrying books from the bindery to the packing room, to selling books retail, to working in the manufacturing department, to finally writing advertising copy. In the late 1880s Doubleday became head of the subscription department. He wanted to create complete uniform sets of the major contemporary authors to be sold by subscription. This would not be an easy task, as various publishers owned the copyrights, and they would have to be persuaded to give them up. Doubleday's first author was Kipling, who was living in Vermont at that time. Having met with Kipling and obtained his enthusiastic support, Doubleday approached the three publishers who owned the copyrights. Macmillan easily granted him permission for eight of Kipling's works, and Appleton for one, but the Century Company, which held copyright for three books, proved very difficult. In the end, however, Doubleday secured the permissions, and the Outward Bound edition of Kipling was offered to subscribers across the nation. It sold in hundreds of thousands of sets. The Scribner subscription sets soon included the works of Robert Louis Stevenson and James M. Barrie, among others.

Doubleday had never had a good relationship with Charles Scribner, head of the firm, and in the mid-1890s he began to think of resigning and founding his own house. Urged on by his wife, he finally told Scribner he was going to resign. Scribner's reaction was to accuse Doubleday of being disloyal and dishonest in taking what he had learned at Scribner's and using it for his own profit. In a fit of anger, Scribner told Doubleday to clear out that afternoon. By the next morning, Scribner had cooled down and, realizing Doubleday's worth, offered him a partnership instead. Doubleday thought it over and decided to refuse. By the next morning Scribner had decided to withdraw his offer, but at the same time Doubleday refused it. Scribner was once again enraged, but Doubleday was well out of it and was now launched on an independent course.

Hearing that Doubleday had left Scribner's, S. S. McClure offered him a job on *McClure's Magazine*. Doubleday then suggested they form a partnership, Doubleday, McClure & Co. One of the first authors acquired by the new firm was Doubleday's old friend Rudyard Kipling, who offered the new firm his next book, *The Day's Work*, which sold over 100,000 copies. The firm lasted only three years, from 1897 to 1900, and was just becoming profitable when Doubleday decided to go it alone.

The new firm was Doubleday, Page & Co., and in spite of the significant contributions of Walter Hines Page, Doubleday was very much in charge. Finally, Doubleday was able to chart his own course and fulfill his ambition to create one of the nation's largest and most prestigious publishing houses. His substantial list grew with the acquisition of McClure's book division in 1908 and the publishing department of Baker and Taylor in 1912. One of his most colorful authors was Mark Twain. At one point Doubleday had arranged for Twain to live near him in New York, and the two men developed a close friendship, though Twain was not always easy to get on with, as Doubleday recounted in his *Memoirs*:

> One day when I was very busy and we were still occupying very small quarters on Sixteenth Street and Union Square, Mark Twain drifted in, smoking a cigar that could be smelled a mile. He insisted upon it that it was a good cigar because he paid seven dollars a barrel for them, but with this I did not agree.
>
> He asked me if I was busy, and I told him that I was. He said to go right on with my work and he would make himself at home for a few

Doubleday was the first of the major publishers to move out of New York. In 1910 he established the Country Life Press in Garden City on Long Island. Occupying 255,000 square feet on 37 acres and including gardens, tennis courts, and pools for its employees, it was a model for the integration of work and leisure far ahead of its time.

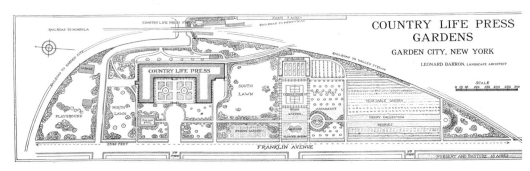

COUNTRY LIFE PRESS GARDENS

GARDEN CITY, NEW YORK

LEONARD BARRON, LANDSCAPE ARCHITECT

minutes. He certainly did. In less time than it takes to write about it almost, he filled the room with a blue smoke, nauseating in its effect, and then he began to look around among the volumes on the shelves. I had in this office some special books which I was carefully keeping for one purpose or another. Mark went around and found a book he wanted, took out a pencil and wrote on the flyleaf, *To my friend, Samuel L. Clemens, with the kind regards of F. N. Doubleday*, put it under his arm, and disappeared.

George Munro established the Seaside Library, a series of uniform cheap reprints, in 1875. A number of other publishers also began issuing libraries in 1875, such as the Lakeside Library published by Donnelley, Lloyd & Co. of Chicago, Norman Munro's Riverside Library, Frank Leslie's Home Library, and Beadle & Adams's Fireside Library. These inexpensive reprints were instantly successful, and by 1877, 2,500,000 copies had been printed. The main-line publishers were hard hit and fought back by establishing their own "libraries," such as Harper & Bros.' Franklin Square Library. By 1883 almost every major title, fiction and nonfiction, had been reprinted, and as a mark of what seemed to be the end, 1,200,000 books from Munro's Seaside Library were returned to the publisher in that year. But the reprinters were not finished. They simply changed formats from paperback to a smaller clothbound volume and reprinted the most popular titles again. By the early 1890s, the impetus of the reprint series was slowing somewhat, but in 1892 it was stopped dead by the adoption of international copyright, which meant the publishers could no longer reprint British and foreign titles without first obtaining copyright permission.

Doubleday was an innovator in his use of advertising. He usually advertised in the major metropolitan newspapers and national magazines, but it was his approach to each book individually that brought him success. He described his approach in the trade magazine *Printer's Ink*:

Each book is its own individual advertising problem, and when you have made a success with one you have hardly any definite principle to put into words or guide you in advertising the next. The only thing about which you can be absolutely certain is that, if you have a reasonably good novel or history or nature book, there are people who will buy it. The problem is to reach and tell them about it, and to do this with as little waste of energy as possible. There is a zest to book publicity that partakes of gambling. You can lose a lot of money in a very short time in book exploitation. From the very first ad that you put out results must be watched, and sometimes the plan of campaign must be changed in a day. There is a factor of the unknown about it. … The chief object is to get people talking about the book. … You must have good goods, your book must be of a certain

MAGNET LIBRARY   NO. 481

The Downward Path
BY
Dick Stewart

STREET & SMITH · PUBLISHERS · NEW YORK

The Downward Path *by Dick Stewart was typical of the dime novels that flooded America in the 1880s, and the house of Street & Smith was one of the most successful publishers of dime novels. When one of Street & Smith's most popular authors, Horatio Alger, Jr., died, the publisher refused to accept that Alger's very profitable series of boys' books had come to an end. Eighteen new titles were published bearing Alger's name, seemingly from beyond the grave.*

literary quality, and you must believe in it.

In 1910 Doubleday left New York and created a new facility in Garden City on Long Island. His Country Life Press occupied 255,000 square feet on 37 acres. It included gardens, tennis courts, and pools for his employees and was a model for the integration of work and leisure far ahead of its time. By the end of the First World War, Frank Doubleday could gaze out across the gardens at the Country Life Press and feel great satisfaction in the fulfillment of his lifetime's ambition to become the nation's leading publisher.

The period from the end of the Civil War to the end of the First World War was a period in which literacy was extended to classes and groups of people who had not heretofore been consumers of books, and as a result the demand for popular entertainment, generally in the form of novels, skyrocketed. In 1873 the second paperback revolution began. Like the first in the 1840s, which had been initiated by the competition between weeklies and publishers, the second revolution was started by a newspaper, the *New York Tribune*, which began to issue "extras" at five to fifteen cents each, followed by the Tribune Novels at ten to twenty cents. Soon the floodgates opened, and by 1886 fully one-third of all books published were issued as cheap paperbacks. The new publishers issued these books in "libraries," series of uniform reprints. The first of these appeared in 1875, the Lakeside Library published by Donnelley, Lloyd & Co. of Chicago. Others included George Munro's Seaside Library, Norman Munro's Riverside Library, Frank Leslie's Home Library, and Beadle & Adams's Fireside Library.

A number of factors allowed these books to be produced at a very low cost. The first was that the paper supply problem had finally been solved with the discovery that paper could be made from wood pulp. Although the use of wood pulp introduced chemical instabilities into paper, it provided an endless supply at very low prices. Perhaps the most significant factor was that there were no royalties to be paid, as the reprints were the pirated works of British or other foreign authors. In addition, all the books in a single library were standardized so that they were of the same size, had the same two or three columns of closely spaced type, and paper covers. Further, technological advances reduced expenses in the printing plant, and, significantly, the Post Office cooperated by charging only two cents per pound (it was cut in half in 1885) to mail the books. But perhaps most important, many of these reprints were proven titles that people wanted to read. As long as publishers stuck to reprints and not new works, there was almost no risk.

By October of 1877 over 2,500,000 of these cheap books had been printed. This immediately forced the regular publishers to lower prices. For example,

By the end of the nineteenth century, advertising was becoming an important part of publishing, though it was considered by some of the grand old men, such as Henry Holt, to be a vulgar pandering to the masses that debased the literary essence of publishing. In 1899 Scribner's Sons issued this poster by Blanch McManus for Frank R. Stockton's Adventures of Captain Horn. *Though little known today, Stockton was one of the most widely admired authors in his own time. He wrote a number of successful romantic adventure novels such as* Captain Horn, *but he also contributed to the newspapers and to magazines such as* Vanity Fair *and served as assistant editor for the children's magazine* St. Nicholas. *He was known to be something of an eccentric who dictated his books while swinging in a hammock. His most enduring work is his story "The Lady or the Tiger?"*

the prices of Harper's Library of Select Novels dropped by about one-third. In the summer of 1878 Harper introduced its own "cheap" library, the Franklin Square Library, modeled on Munro's Seaside Library. At first the reprinters confined themselves to fiction, with the result that the mainstream publishers were unable to publish a copyrighted novel at a profit, but at least nonfiction remained untouched. Soon, however, as the supply of popular novels, even those translated from other languages, had been exhausted, the reprinters were forced to turn to nonfiction. By 1883 there was little left to reprint, and the public was buying fewer and fewer of the reprints. Munro had 1,200,000 books from his Seaside Library returned in that year. As a result, most of the reprinters changed formats from the somewhat large paperbacks to a smaller clothbound volume (though every bit as cheap). These proved popular, and now the reprinters could work their way through the most popular titles again. In 1886 alone nearly 1,500 new titles were reprinted, and the competition between reprint houses was intense. Some of the reprinters had their own plants, known as "saw mills," where a cheap novel could be turned out in ten hours in vast quantity, though extraordinarily poor quality.

As new titles to pirate became scarcer and scarcer, some firms set up fiction factories to turn out suitable stories. The Nick Carter series proved so successful for Street & Smith that the production schedule was moved up from monthly to weekly. Its author, Frederick Dey, found himself unable to produce a novel a week, but the publisher simply found an additional five authors to ghostwrite for him, all the novels appearing with Dey's name and the public apparently still quite satisfied. When one of Street & Smith's most popular authors, Horatio Alger, Jr., died, Edward Stratemeyer, one of the fiction factory writers, produced eighteen more titles under Alger's name. One cannot help but speculate on how the public received these additional titles as if from beyond the grave. By 1892, however, production costs were up, profit margins down, and the public seemed increasingly dissatisfied with poor-quality books. It was the adoption of the international copyright law that year, however, that put an end to piracy reprints and the second paperback revolution. Cheap books continued to be published, but they no longer dominated the scene. It would be the late 1930s and early 1940s before the next paperback boom.

Advertising and promotion had long been viewed with distaste within the trade. Since the early decades of the nineteenth century, publishers had sent out review copies and had endeavored to ensure favorable reviews, but overt advertising was quite a different thing. Attempts at advertising were often inept. In 1885 an editorial in the *New York Times* noted, "Authors frequently complain that their books do not sell, and they do not understand the reason for this unpleasant state of things. The reason is plain. Publishers have no real conception of the art of advertising ... and consequently few books sell." Many publishers, led by Henry Holt, thought they understood advertising quite well, and they wanted none of it. But attitudes finally began to change in the 1890s. Funk & Wagnalls had been advertising on streetcars in the 1880s, and some publishers employed "sandwich men" to announce new novels. In the 1890s Doubleday tried some innovative advertising; for example, an advertisement for one of Ellen Glasgow's books appeared each day containing one additional letter of the title until it had been fully spelled out. The first full-scale advertising campaign for a book was probably mounted in 1898 with Charles Major's *When Knighthood Was in Flower*. Full-page advertisements were displayed in magazines that compared the author, whose name was not revealed, to such literary greats as Shakespeare, Scott, Dumas, and others. The public was fascinated, and the publisher encouraged highly publicized attempts to discover the author's name. Sales were huge, and the publishing world was duly impressed. Advertising was here to stay, and with it the publishing industry firmly entered the twentieth century.

The Armed Services Editions provided quality literature and recreational reading for millions of American service-men and women during World War II and the immediate postwar years. Between 1943 and 1947 almost 123 million copies of 1,322 titles were issued. The product of a cooperative effort between the American book trade and the War Department, these paperbacks were eagerly snapped up by enthusiastic readers overseas. The Armed Services Editions took their distinctive wide form from their mode of production. Because they were printed on rotary presses, usually devoted to producing magazines, two books, together equaling the size of a normal magazine, were printed at a time, one book above the other, and then cut in half, yielding two wide paperbacks.

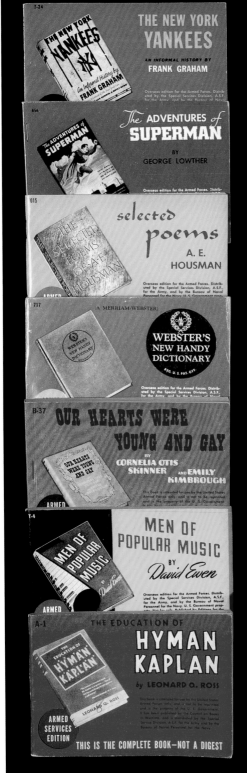

Books at War

From at least the time of the Civil War, books have provided soldiers with countless hours of entertainment and edification. A soldier's life is one of almost endless tedium punctuated by short periods of intense activity. It was during the long hours in camp that soldiers eagerly devoured any books that might come their way. During the Civil War, various religious organizations provided the Union Army with portable libraries, and, in addition, soldiers consumed millions of copies of Beadle's Dime Novels, many semi-literate soldiers reading whole books for the first time in their lives. Such habits stayed with the returning veterans and accelerated the spread of literacy and promoted the habit of reading. During the First World War the American Library Association, working with a number of other organizations such as the YMCA, established training-camp libraries. The Library War Service program lasted well after the end of the war, and by 1920 the ALA had raised over $5 million, built thirty-six training-camp libraries with funds from the Carnegie Corporation, distributed about ten million books and periodicals, and provided library services to over five thousand locations. The Library War Service was so successful that it led to the establishment of permanent military libraries. With America's entry into World War II in 1941, the military library system grew to over one thousand post and hospital libraries. Almost every navy ship had a library, and Armed Services Editions were made available to troops overseas. Military libraries continue to be an integral part of the American armed services.

By June 1918 there was an average of more than twenty-five thousand volumes in each of the major ALA-sponsored camp libraries. Each library received fifty-one magazines, and, in addition, the public donated more than five million magazines to the camp libraries through an ingenious plan adopted by the post office. Once finished with a magazine, readers could affix a one-cent stamp to the cover and the post office would deliver it to one of the camp libraries. The library buildings were standard army wood construction, which were provided with good lighting and coal-burning stoves for heat in the winter. Each library was supplied with a telephone and a vehicle, pictured here, which was used to get books out to eager readers. Vancouver Barracks (Washington), ca. 1918.

The ALA training-camp libraries were quite successful and very popular with the soldiers. One army sergeant, upon first visiting the library at Camp Funston (Kansas), exclaimed, "I'll be hanged if this isn't civilization!" The libraries were heavily used: On a Tuesday evening in April 1918 more than 320 soldiers crowded into the library at Camp Greene (North Carolina), and at Camp Kearny (California) more than 1,000 soldiers used the library in a single day. Pictured here is ALA librarian Elizabeth J. Herrington together with her avid readers in the camp library, Vancouver Barracks, ca. 1918.

Horace Liveright was without doubt the most colorful publisher in New York in the 1920s. Liveright was famous for his ability to perceive a potential bestseller without actually reading the manuscript, and his list of authors included such greats as Faulkner, Hemingway, Sherwood Anderson, Dreiser, O'Neill, George Moore, Gertrude Atherton, Robinson Jeffers, Hendrik Willem Van Loon, Rose Macaulay, and Sigmund Freud. His lifestyle was very much a part of the age, but with the Crash in 1929 he lost control of his firm, and after an abortive attempt to break into Holly-wood, he returned to New York a broken man. After Liveright's death in 1931, Sherwood Anderson said, "It was all rather crazy, rather splendid. Horace was a gambler, and if he believed in you, he would gamble on you. I have always thought, since the man's death, that too much emphasis has been put on the reckless splendor of the man rather than on his never-ending generosity and his real belief in men of talent." Frontispiece photo-graph from Walker Gilmer's Horace Liveright: Publisher of the Twenties *(New York: David Lewis, 1970).*

V
The Book in
Twentieth-Century America

After the First World War, America retreated into a self-absorption and fascination with American culture that in many ways rejected the internationalism fostered during the war. Though the literary and publishing scene, especially in New York, was less isolationist than the rest of the country, the prevailing trends and attitudes created a hot-house effect that both stimulated the business climate and shaped the national cultural landscape. The decade following the war has been variously described as the Jazz Age, the Roaring Twenties, and the Era of Wonderful Opportunity, and for the publishing industry this last appellation is perhaps the most apt. All business had suffered to some degree through the postwar depression, but by 1921 the publisher George Doran was able to proclaim: "Never in the history of literature in America has there been such an increase in the number of readers, or ... so widespread an interest in all kinds of books. ... We are on the threshold of a new American era of novels, plays, and poetry." The grand old men of the last generation were still a force, but it was a conservative force that looked on the new generation of publishers with distaste and even alarm. At the beginning of the decade, Henry Holt celebrated his eightieth birthday and Edward P. Dutton his ninetieth. Holt was writing his memoirs, *Garrulities of an Octogenarian Editor*, which was being serialized in his magazine, the *Unpartizan Review* (formerly the *Unpopular Review*). The new generation, however, was not to be denied.

Prominent among the new generation was Albert Boni. Boni and his brother Charles began as booksellers in Greenwich Village with the Washington Square Book Shop in 1912. The shop soon became a meeting place for writers, actors, artists, and anyone involved in the cultural life of the city. The Theatre Guild was founded there, and the shop hosted the Guild's first production. The shop also soon became a meeting place for liberal and radical political activists such as Emma Goldman, John Reed, Margaret Sanger, Theodore Dreiser, and Bill Heywood. At about the same time, the Bonis initiated their first publishing venture, the Little Leather Library,

121

F. Scott Fitzgerald first came to notice in 1920 with the publication of his first novel, This Side of Paradise, *a brilliant and witty work that captured the essence of the postwar Jazz Age. Indeed, it was Fitzgerald who coined the term "Jazz Age," and he essentially invented the flapper and the sheik in his fiction. His greatest novel,* The Great Gatsby, *was published in 1925 and confirmed his stature and reputation as one of America's leading novelists. Fitzgerald's life seemed to mirror the boom and bust of the 1920s. With the Crash of 1929 and the end of the Jazz Age, Fitzgerald lost his subject, but out of his personal despair came his second great novel,* Tender Is the Night. *He explained that his early success had been "unnatural—unnatural as the Boom. … My recent experience parallels the wave of despair that swept the nation when the Boom was over." Photograph by Carl Van Vechten, 1937.*

which consisted of thirty reprinted classics bound in imitation limp leather. They were marketed as a set by mail and sold for $2.98 per volume. Soon, however, the brothers found their financial situation difficult, and they sold both the Little Leather Library and the Washington Square Book Shop.

In late 1916 Albert Boni was making a living in an advertising agency, and there he had the great good fortune to meet Horace Liveright. Boni told Liveright about his idea for a series of books devoted to modern European classics. Liveright was immediately enthusiastic, and the two men formed a partnership, Boni & Liveright, to publish the series. The series was announced in the spring of 1917 as the Modern Library of the World's Best Classics, which was quickly shortened to the Modern Library. Eighteen titles, all reprints, were issued with great success. These reprints were followed by original works by Leon Trotsky and Theodore Dreiser. Other titles included works by Wilde, Strindberg, Ibsen, France, Maupassant, Nietzsche, Dostoyevsky, Maeterlinck, Schopenhauer, and many others. The series proved quite successful, as it made many of its authors widely available to the American public for the first time.

The old mainstream publishers looked rather askance at this new firm with its leftist leanings and sometimes radical list. After the entrance of the United States into the war, and in the face of great enthusiasm and patriotism across the country, Boni & Liveright brought out pacifist works by Trotsky, Andreas Latzko, and Henri Barbusse. Latzko's *Men in War* was suppressed by the government in June 1918, and the firm was even kept under surveillance. Though the partners shared a common political outlook, they found themselves unable to agree on anything else. In July 1918 Boni and Liveright agreed that the partnership should end, but they could not decide who should become the majority owner and control the firm. Finally, they decided to flip a coin, and Liveright won. The Boni brothers went into publishing for themselves; Liveright continued as Boni & Liveright until 1928 and thereafter as Horace Liveright, Inc.

By 1924 Liveright had an exceptional list that included Dreiser, O'Neill, Sherwood Anderson, George Moore, Gertrude Atherton, Ludwig Lewisohn, Robinson Jeffers, Hendrik Willem Van Loon, Rose Macaulay, and Sigmund Freud. The Modern Library was selling well, and the firm had an income of over $1 million that year. Liveright was at the center of the literary, theatrical, and art scene in the 1920s and had that instinct, so necessary for a successful publisher, of knowing a bestseller when he saw it, in spite of the fact that he rarely read a manuscript or a book. He was one of the first to recognize the talents of Faulkner, Hemingway, Sherwood Anderson, Ben Hecht, and Liam O'Flaherty. In publishing Anita Loos's *Gentlemen Prefer Blondes*, he knew he had a major bestseller. But counterbalanced to this was his profligate spending and chaotic business dealings. Bennett Cerf, who came to work for Liveright in 1924, observed:

> Seven men in the organization had authority to turn in bills for "entertainment." Authors in the waiting room were often outnumbered by bootleggers. … The head bookkeeper (the only real business man in the place, as he proved convincingly by winding up … as the sole owner of the entire outfit) had to show a perpetual deficit in his daily reports to the president, because if there ever was a cash balance it was gone by nightfall.

In spite of Liveright's brilliant list and his uncanny literary instincts, the firm was being run into the ground. The various departments often carried on without consulting each other, the results being costly errors. For example, *Gentlemen Prefer Blondes* was first priced at $2 but then reduced to $1.75 without consulting the manufacturing department. The bestseller sold hundreds of thousands of copies, but because it was priced below what it cost to manufacture, each copy lost money. This was no way to do business.

Right from the start Liveright had attracted a number of bright and promising young men and women to work for him. Many such as Lillian Hellman, Manuel Komroff, Louis Kronenberger, Leane Zugsmith, Edward Weeks, Isidor Schneider, David Ross, and Julian Messner were to go on to make their own marks in publishing in the years to come. Perhaps the two most noted young men to work with Liveright were Richard Simon, who left to found Simon and Schuster, and Bennett

Cerf, who bought the Modern Library from Liveright and left to establish Random House. By 1928 almost all had left for promising careers elsewhere. Still, Liveright continued to attract new bright young people, his list was stellar, and in spite of it all he continued his profligate ways with parties, women, and risky theatrical investments. It was the Crash of 1929 that wiped out his fortune, not his chaotic business practices. Liveright borrowed heavily from Arthur Pell, his bookkeeper, exchanging stock for cash, and soon found that Pell controlled the firm. Pell ended the parties and all the extravagances, but it only delayed the inevitable. Liveright tried to make a go of it in Hollywood but soon returned to New York and to the firm that bore his name. After a number of visits, Pell exclaimed to him, "Horace, I don't think you'd better come in anymore; it doesn't look well for business." He left silently and never returned. In the fall of 1931 he died of pneumonia. Bennett Cerf wrote:

> A straggling handful of people gathered in the Universal Chapel yesterday morning while Upton Sinclair, fearfully embarrassed, mumbled inadequate nothings over the last remains of Horace Liveright, dead at 49. Most of the authors he had started on the road to success, and the friends for whom he had neglected his business when it needed him most, were far too busy to spare the few moments necessary to pay him a last tribute. It was a dismal last curtain to a spectacular career—and to a publisher whose like will never be seen again. …

If there was one publisher Liveright envied more than any other, it was Alfred A. Knopf. Knopf had entered the trade at about the same time as Liveright, establishing his publishing house in 1915. He had quickly established the firm, with its distinctive imprint of a borzoi dog, as the embodiment of both literary quality and fine book production. In 1926 The *New Yorker* said of him: "Alfred Knopf has a savant's taste for and judgment of good literature, an enormous self-confidence which makes him back these tastes to the limit, a ruthless energy which makes realization out of ideas." He was joined by his father, Samuel Knopf, known as S. K., who handled the business end of things, and by his wife, Blanche, in 1918, who became vice president and head of the editorial department. In the same *New Yorker* piece, she was described as "young, exotic, and charming. … She takes [authors] to lunch, has them to her home for dinner, and gives them the sense that they are being well taken care of by competent publishers." The three Knopfs proved to be a formidable team.

Alfred Knopf concentrated on and attracted the nation's, and indeed the world's, best authors. He was especially concerned with the design and physical production of the book. Many of the nation's best craftsmen and designers worked for Knopf, including Frederic Goudy, Bruce Rogers, W. A. Dwiggins, Warren Chappell, and others. George Doran noted that Knopf "not only made beautiful books but told the public they were beautiful books and thereby stimulated the public to require a more graceful format." Certainly, authors were attracted to Knopf because of his attention to the details of type, paper, and binding in a way that combined all the elements of the physical book into a sympathetic reflection of the subject matter. The sum of the author's text and the publisher's treatment of the physical book produced a totality that continues to this day as an ideal for literary publishing.

Alfred A. Knopf's vision of the book has exerted a tremendous influence on American publishing in the twentieth century. He was especially concerned with the design and physical production of the book, and many of the nation's best designers worked for Knopf, including Frederic Goudy, Bruce Rogers, W. A. Dwiggins, and Warren Chappell. Photograph by Carl Van Vechten, March 31, 1935.

By 1925 Knopf's list included T. S. Eliot, Thomas Mann, André Gide, Sigrid Undset, Knut Hamsun, D. H. Lawrence, Willa Cather, Katherine Mansfield, Carl Van Vechten, H. L. Mencken, Walter de la Mare, David Garnett, Frank Swinnerton, Francis Brett Young, Elinor Wylie, and Hilaire Belloc, to name but a few. The list was controlled by Knopf's wide-ranging interests and his taste. As a result of his interest in food and wine, the firm published G. B. Stern, André Simon, and Julian Street. Due to his passion for music, the memoirs of Berlioz and Rimsky-Korsakov were secured and published. Wherever his interests ranged, authors and books followed. And each book was individually important to him. Sidney R. Jacobs, who headed the production department for many years, recalled, "I became aware of Alfred's involvement in every phase of design and manufacturing. Every layout and design, including a final pasted-up folder of front matter proof and typical text pages that eventually went to the printer as a pressroom guide, every jacket design, every binding layout and setup and sample cover had to be submitted to Alfred for approval."

As the decade approached its end, the publishing industry had reason to be optimistic about the future. Sales were at a record high. In 1928 a new trend toward

In the summer of 1935 in a kitchen in Akron, Ohio, two men struggling to control their drinking created the beginnings of an organization that would come to be known as Alcoholics Anonymous. Over the next few years these two, known as Dr. Bob and Bill W., produced a book that set out the fundamental twelve steps of the AA program. Alcoholics Anonymous, *known as the "Big Book," was published in 1939. Its first edition sold over 300,000 copies in sixteen years, and the second edition, published in 1955, sold over 1,150,000 copies. It is now in its third edition and has been translated into twenty-six languages. The twelve-step program pioneered by AA has been used and adapted by many other groups across the nation and has had an extraordinary effect on many Americans.*

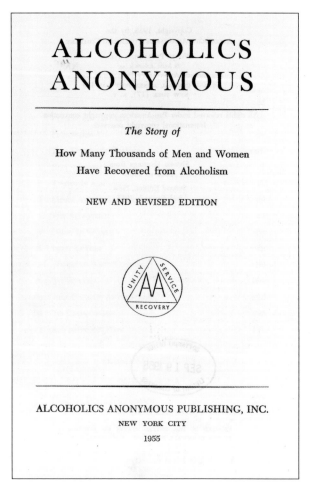

ALCOHOLICS ANONYMOUS

The Story of

How Many Thousands of Men and Women Have Recovered from Alcoholism

NEW AND REVISED EDITION

ALCOHOLICS ANONYMOUS PUBLISHING, INC.
NEW YORK CITY
1955

nonfiction by the trade publishers was much in evidence, and publishers were finally coming around to the view that book clubs actually stimulated sales and were generally a good thing. The output of books for the first half of 1929 was up and looked to continue for the indefinite future. However, that was not to be, as the stock market crash in October of that year caught everyone off guard. At first many in the trade would not believe what was happening. George Brett reassured his fellow publishers when he pronounced that the trade "may look forward to 1930 with every confidence," and Bennett Cerf added, "I think that all this talk about depression is a lot of baloney."

In spite of such assessments the Depression continued to deepen, but the publishing business was not as hard hit as many other segments of industry. One response to the downturn was to lower book prices in the hope of attracting greater sales. In 1930 Simon and Schuster, Coward-McCann, and Farrar & Rinehart lowered prices for fiction titles from $2 or $2.50 to $1. This caused a great outcry of protest from other publishers, but in 1933 Knopf and Dutton also reduced prices. By 1933 only two firms had gone under, one being Liveright, though a number had reorganized and most had restricted their lists. As a general response to the Depression, most firms lowered overhead costs, reduced salaries and paid vacations, eliminated expense accounts, reduced the number of books published, lowered prices, and reduced profit margins. As a result, the industry came through the Depression in relatively good shape.

The third paperback revolution was initiated by Robert de Graff in 1939. De Graff had started with Doubleday, Page in 1922 and by 1925 was vice president and director of Garden City Publishing, a Doubleday subsidiary. In the mid-thirties he became president of the reprint house Blue Ribbon Books but soon resigned to design a new and inexpensive book, one that would be "pleasing to the eye and agreeable to the touch." He said, "I am convinced that the mass American public wants the best in books ... at irresistibly low prices, with almost universal distribution." De Graff examined other inexpensive paperback reprints, such as the British Penguins, and in the summer of 1938 he issued one thousand copies of a trial edition of Pearl Buck's *The Good Earth*. These were sent out to a sample of readers who were asked if they would spend a quarter for such a book. In addition he sent out a survey to forty-nine thousand other readers. His responses were overwhelmingly positive, and the first Pocket Books were published on June 19, 1939. A full-page ad in the *New York Times* announced:

> The New Pocket Books that may revolutionize New York's reading habits. Today is the most important literary coming-out party in the memory of New York's oldest book lover. Today your 25¢ piece leaps to a par with dollar bills. Now for less than the few cents you spend each week for your morning newspaper you can own one of the great books for which thousands of people have paid from $2 to $4. These new Pocket Books are designed to fit both the tempo of our times and the needs of New Yorkers. They're as handy as a pencil, as modern and convenient as a portable radio—and as good looking. They were designed specially for busy people—people who are continually on the go, yet who want to make the most of every minute. Never again need you say "I wish I had time to read" because Pocket Books gives you the time. Never again need you dawdle idly in reception rooms, fret on train or bus rides, sit vacantly staring at a restaurant table. The books you have always meant to read "when you had time" will fill the waits with enjoyment.

The first ten titles included a range of works such as *Five Great Tragedies* by Shakespeare, *The Bridge of San Luis Rey, Lost Horizon, Topper*, Agatha Christie's *The Murder of Roger Ackroyd*, and *Bambi*, among others. De Graff's partners were Richard Simon, Max Schuster, and Leon Shimkin, three of the nation's most astute publishers, but on June 19 even they were unprepared for the public response to Pocket Books. By noon large reorders were coming in, not only from bookstores and department stores, but from newsstands and cigar stores. Soon the orders were flooding in from drugstores and variety stores, and the initial print runs of 10,000 copies were exhausted within a week. By the end of 1939, 1,500,000 copies had been shipped. The inexpensive Pocket Books had discovered a whole new reading public: people

The modern paperback revolution began in America with Robert de Graff's Pocket Books in 1939. With their phenomenal success, other paperback publishers soon began issuing titles and distributing them through drugstores and newsstands rather than bookstores. A spin-off of a magazine publisher, Dell began in 1942, guided by Helen Meyer, and has remained a major paperback publisher to this day. In 1957 Dell changed paperback publishing forever with its blockbuster bestseller Peyton Place. *The success of* Peyton Place *propelled Dell to new heights and with it the whole paperback publishing sector. As a mark of that success Dell launched its own hardback imprints, Dial and Delacorte, in the 1960s. Dell was acquired by Doubleday in 1976.*

who had never ventured into bookstores and who would never consider paying $2 for a book, but who were quite willing to pay a quarter for a book at the local drugstore. Pocket books were soon to be found across the nation, literally in everyone's pocket.

Success was ensured in mid-1940 when Pocket Books published Dale Carnegie's *How to Win Friends and Influence People.* Carnegie's self-help book had been a great bestseller for Simon and Schuster, and de Graff had to convince his partners, Simon, Schuster, and Shimkin, that paperback sales would not have an adverse effect on their hardcover sales. Wallis Howe, sales manager for Pocket, recounted how de Graff approached his three partners:

> De Graff opened his big blue eyes and I kind of felt sorry for the three Esses [Simon, Schuster, and Shimkin] because they didn't know what was about to hit them. "I don't want you fellows to take any risk whatsoever, so let's make a test. We'll take the toughest sales area in the country— Texas. … We can hardly hope to win, but I think we owe it to you."

Unknown to the three Esses, one of the firm's largest accounts was an extensive Texas drug chain, and in addition the firm's leading distributor in Texas specialized in drugstores. This emphasis on drugstores, which were more heavily concentrated in Texas than in any other state, ensured wide distribution to many people who would never have purchased a hardcover copy of Carnegie's bestseller but were more than eager to get the book for a mere quarter. Following the successful test, the book was distributed nationwide, and sales from this one title equaled the income received from all other titles combined.

In 1941 Pocket Books initiated a new method of distribution that created the first true mass distribution system for books. Early in the year Pocket managed to get four independent wholesale distributors to carry Pocket Books. These distributors sold magazines and tabloids to newsstands, drugstores, groceries, and variety stores. It was a ready-made distribution system for the inexpensive paperbacks. Initially the distributors were hesitant, but by the end of the year most of the nation's seven hundred distributors were moving the books into over 100,000 retail outlets. *Time* magazine noted that in Columbus, Ohio, trade books could be purchased in 6 bookstores, while Pocket Books could be purchased at 224 outlets. These independent distributors have remained the major avenue for distribution of mass-market paperbacks, accounting for about two-thirds of sales.

What de Graff had done was to bring together a number of elements, none of which was new, to create a new segment of the publishing industry that in time would come to challenge the old-line trade houses. He opted to publish popular titles, a lesson Parson Weems had taught Matthew Carey. He adopted the paperback format, which was well established and had a long history. He used attractive cover illustrations, a practice at least as old as the dime novels of the previous century. He utilized high-speed production techniques that had been used for some time to produce magazines. He adopted a distribution system that had been in place for nearly a century, but which brought books to the mass market for the first time. What he brought to this combination was a solid background in publishing, a brilliant idea, and a driving vision. With the respectable backing of Simon and Schuster, de Graff laid the foundation for a major shift in American publishing.

De Graff was soon challenged by a number of competing firms. One month after Pocket Books was launched, Ian Ballantine returned from England to set up an American office for Penguin Books. By the fall of 1940 Ballantine was producing Penguins in the United States and a year later was even shipping them to England. However, the first major American challenger to Pocket Books was Avon Books. Avon was established by Joseph Meyers in the fall of 1941 with the backing of the American News Company. Pocket sued Avon for copying its format, but in 1944 the court ruled in Avon's favor. Even before the court decision, others entered the field: Dell Books and Popular Library, both backed by major magazine publishers, began issuing paperbacks in 1943.

In 1945 Ian Ballantine left Penguin to organize and direct Bantam Books, which was backed by Grosset & Dunlap and by the magazine publisher and distributor Curtis Publishing. Ballantine intended to challenge Pocket Books directly. He was able to obtain the rights to reprint such American authors as Steinbeck, Hemingway, and Fitzgerald, which put Bantam on the road to success. When Ballantine departed from Penguin, he had left Kurt Enoch, who was soon joined by Victor Weybright. By the end of 1947 Enoch and Weybright managed to negotiate the rights for all the Penguin and Pelican titles that had originated from the American office, and with these rights they left Penguin and formed a new company, the New American Library of World Literature (NAL). NAL established two imprints, Signet and Mentor, and its first book, Faulkner's *The Wild Palms*, appeared in 1948. From this very respectable start, NAL built up its list to the point that it was able to compete directly with Pocket Books in the mid-1950s. In the late 1940s Fawcett Publications, a magazine publisher and distributor, was distributing NAL titles but was forbidden by contract to publish its own reprints. However, Fawcett was not prohibited from publishing new titles as paperbacks, and this is exactly what it did in 1950, much to the consternation of the publishing community. Authors, on the other hand, were quite delighted with this development. Fawcett was willing to give an author an immediate $3,000 cash advance, in contrast to the traditional hardcover publishers, who delayed paying royalties until after a certain number of volumes had been sold. Naturally, other paperback publishers including Dell, Avon, and Popular Library, followed suit, and by 1955 one-third of all paperback titles were original works.

In 1952, Ian Ballantine was again on the move. He left Bantam to found Ballantine Books, where he implemented a new scheme. He offered authors advances of about $5,000 and guaranteed both soft and hardcover publication. Such arrangements had several advantages for the traditional trade publishers, who would publish a hardcover edition simultaneously with Ballantine's paperback edition. Because both publishers could use the same printing plates, production costs were reduced. In addition, the hardcover publisher was guaranteed royalties from the paperback sales. Ballantine's scheme met with only limited success, and so he went on to publish his own hardcover editions, a first for a paperback house. In any case, authors were now turning to the paperback publishers, and those who published with the traditional houses began to demand guarantees of paperback publication. The paperback market was becoming a major force in publishing.

In time, the response of the trade houses was to enter the paperback market and compete with the mass-market publishers, though not directly. Doubleday's Anchor Books, begun in 1953, was the first major trade paperback series to be established by an old-line house. Anchor targeted serious readers and in particular college students for course-related titles. Such works as Stendhal's *The Charterhouse of Parma*, D. H. Lawrence's *Studies in Classic American Literature*, and David Riesman's *The Lonely Crowd* were sold at an average price of seventy-five cents. Other trade houses followed suit with Knopf's Vintage Books, Dutton's Everyman Paperbacks, and Viking's Compass Books, among many others. A more direct and effective response to the explosion in mass-market paperbacks was to acquire a mass-market house. Simon and Schuster acquired Pocket Books, Random House acquired Ballantine Books, and Doubleday acquired Dell.

When the first paperback publishers appeared on the publishing scene, they were looked down upon by the established trade houses. Victor Weybright, of Penguin, recounted how Dodd, Mead had planned to honor George Bernard Shaw's ninetieth birthday in 1946: "When I told Howard Lewis of Dodd, Mead that I thought that we should be in on the celebration, which was to take place at the Waldorf-Astoria, he looked at our paperback editions of *Saint Joan, Pygmalion* and *Major Barbara* and suggested that we have our own party at the Automat." Such arrogance could not be maintained for long in the face of the huge sales figures being piled up by the unpretentious paperbacks. In 1949, 175 million paperbacks were sold, and by 1952 that figure had increased to 250 million. The paperback publishers were quickly moving into a position of independence. Had the celebration of Shaw's birthday taken place ten years later, there can be no doubt that the paperback publishers would have been well in evidence at the Waldorf-Astoria.

At the end of World War II, the old traditional firms looked to the future with optimism. Perhaps they should have seen the mass-market paperback explosion in the future. This was the third such "revolution" to rock the publishing industry in a little over a century, but the established houses could ultimately deal with such an upheaval. After all, it was a crisis within the trade. What was totally unexpected was the takeover of virtually all the major houses by larger corporations, organizations with no understanding or respect for the traditions of publishing and whose major motivation was profit. With this act the long shift away from an individualistic publisher who was sensitive to literary and cultural issues was nearly complete.

Mergers and takeovers were nothing new in the publishing industry, but they had almost always been internal to the trade, one publisher taking over a smaller house and the like. By the end of the 1950s it was becoming obvious that the nature of the industry was changing. The venerable house of Henry Holt & Co. had been merged into Holt, Rinehart & Winston and was no longer controlled by anyone with publishing experience. Soon the pace quickened as Meridian Books was acquired

Rachel Carson in 1963, just after appearing before the United States Senate to warn of the "contamination of the environment." Carson was a marine biologist who had already written two bestsellers, The Sea Around Us *in 1951 and* The Edge of the Sea *in 1955.*

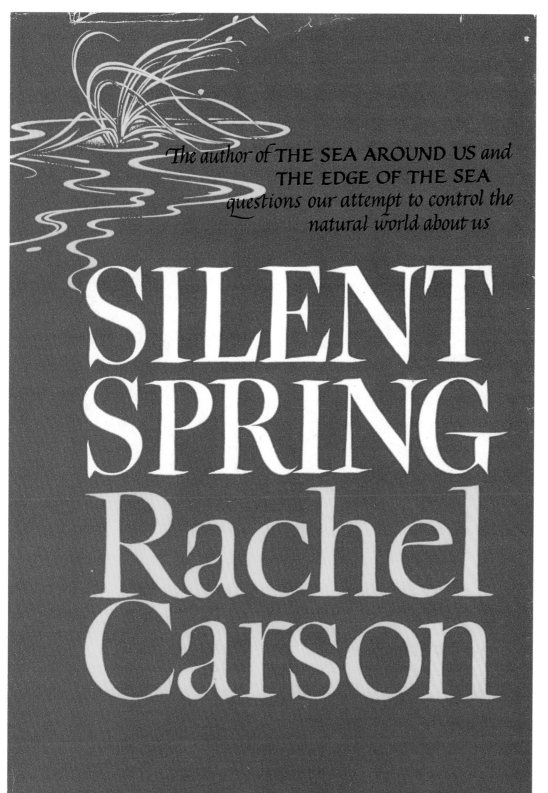

Silent Spring *appeared in 1962, a surprise bestseller that sold 500,000 copies in hardback and millions in paper. Although the book was primarily concerned with the misuse of pesticides, it was the first work to address the larger issues of environmental pollution. Published by Houghton Mifflin,* Silent Spring *remained on the bestseller list for thirty-one weeks and catapulted Carson to national prominence. When she died in 1963, the* New York Times *characterized her as "one of the most influential women of her time."*

Ralph Nader testifying before the Joint Economic Committee of Congress, August 20, 1971. Nader gained national attention in 1965 as an expert on auto safety with the publication of Unsafe at Any Speed. *In 1966 he testified before Congress, and his testimony was influential in the passage of the National Traffic and Motor Vehicle Safety Act, which brought car design under federal control. Nader was also instrumental in the passage of legislation on matters such as food safety, radiation hazards, and natural gas pipeline safety. By 1969 the activities of his informal group of followers, called "Nader's Raiders," led to the establishment of the Center for Study of Responsive Law and in 1971 to the establishment of Public Citizen, Inc. In the 1980s Nader concentrated on the insurance industry and promoted the provision of automobile air bags. Nader and his associates, and many other Nader-inspired organizations, continue to monitor Congress and the activities of large corporations, lobby for new legislation, and undertake legal action. Photograph by Warren K. Loeffler.*

UNSAFE AT ANY SPEED

The designed-in dangers of the American automobile

Ralph Nader

Grossman Publishers

NEW YORK ●● 1965

by World; NAL by the Times-Mirror Corporation; Knopf by Random House; and then Random House by RCA. At the same time, a number of firms went public, foremost among them Western Publishing; Houghton Mifflin; Harcourt, Brace; and Random House. In the next round, Fawcett, Praeger, and Saunders were acquired by CBS (which already owned Popular Library and Holt, Rinehart & Winston); Simon and Schuster and Prentice-Hall were acquired by Gulf & Western (now Paramount Communications); RCA sold Random House to Newhouse Newspapers; Putnam (which had previously acquired Berkley), Jove Books, and Coward, McCann & Geoghegan were acquired by MCA; Ace Books and Grosset & Dunlap by Filmways; and William Morrow & Co. and Arbor House by Hearst, which had earlier acquired Avon. Between 1958 and 1970 there were over three hundred mergers. During the peak years from 1965 to 1969 there were at least twenty-three mergers a year, forty-seven in 1968. Very few publishing houses were unaffected, and some were acquired and sold several times. Few of the houses were able to withstand the trend, but one notable exception was McGraw-Hill, itself a publishing conglomerate. In 1979 American Express attempted to take over McGraw-Hill in a sharp battle. Harold McGraw organized a stubborn resistance, in spite of a sizable number of stockholders who favored the deal, and stopped American Express. Such success was rare.

John Tebbel, the eminent historian of American publishing, has suggested that the publishing trade, as it has endured from the time of Isaiah Thomas and Matthew Carey, has been so transformed in the past few decades that it is no longer recognizable. Writing in 1985, he surveyed the contemporary scene and found that the most notable change was that the fun had gone out of publishing. This may seem to be a particularly frivolous statement, but in fact it gets right to the heart of the transformation of the trade. Tebbel explained that historically publishing's "chief ingredient was a love of the printed page, of the book. People in publishing liked the feel of the book in hand, and they were almost all inveterate readers, from the publisher himself on down. The joy of finding a manuscript that was deemed worthy of publication was shared by everyone involved. When readers felt the same way, those who had made it possible were delighted. If it failed in the marketplace, there was some sorrow, but seldom regret for having published it. … Publishing, in short, was like a small town where everyone knew everyone else and felt a kinship that was not to be found in ordinary commercial enterprises." With the takeovers of the large houses, the sense of community, centered on a tradition that emphasized literature, books, and culture, was disrupted and even suppressed. Even those firms that had resisted takeovers were affected. An article on Houghton Mifflin in the *Wall Street Journal* in 1980 summed up the situation when a new trade book manager was brought in

Just before Jack Kerouac died in 1969, he told Neal Cassady that he feared he would die like Melville, unknown and unappreciated in his own time. Kerouac published his first novel in 1950 but came to wider notice with On the Road *in 1957.* On the Road *has become a classic of the Beat Movement with its stream-of-consciousness depiction of the rejection of mainstream American values set in a physical and metaphysical journey across America. Kerouac claimed to have written the novel in an intensive three-week period, and contemporary critics were at something of a loss as to what it all meant, finally declaring Kerouac and the Beat Movement to be un-American, anti-intellec-tual, and drug crazed. But many others embraced Kerouac and the Beats and found a pacifist and spiri-tual message in* On the Road *and particularly in* The Dharma Bums *(1958), which continued the journey, but emphasized the quest for illumination through Zen Buddhism. Kerouac wrote a number of other novels, but these two remain his best known and most influential. When he died in 1969, he was still a marginal author, and he had reason to fear he might suffer "the curse of Melville," but his novels have demonstrated staying power and his road remains well traveled.*

who had no book experience. "The old-line editors who founded and long ran publishing houses are being replaced in top managerial jobs by a new breed, the professional manager. More and more houses have been acquired by big companies with a gimlet eye on the bottom line. Houghton, one of the best-known remaining independents, has had to bow to the new realities." Even the nation's bookstores have been conglomerated into a few large chains that have the ability to control the success or failure of any trade book simply by accepting or rejecting a title for distribution.

If the situation appears bleak for the major old-line houses, the situation away from the center is quite different. Smaller presses and publishers have flourished for years but generally have had little impact on mainstream trade publishing. However, with the advent of new computer-based technologies that have enabled almost anyone to become a publisher, new publishing houses have sprung up all over the country. Many have highly specialized lists that serve a narrow group of readers well, usually through direct marketing. Others have more generalized yet focused lists and sell in the traditional markets. These new houses are almost all located away from the traditional urban centers such as New York, and many are located on the West Coast. Whereas in the past it was necessary to be situated in New York, or one of a few other urban centers, for both cultural and business reasons, this is no longer so. New York's importance as a cultural center and distribution hub has diminished, and at the same time it has become an extraordinarily expensive city in which to conduct business. This has created further problems for the old-line houses and their corporate owners, but at the same time it has created opportunities for the new houses. And in spite of the dominance of the large bookstore chains, independent bookstores are also appearing and flourishing up and down the country.

Is there a crisis in publishing? It seems there has always been a crisis of one kind or another, and perhaps when seen in historical context it is possible to imagine that this particular crisis is not the end of a noble trade but simply a reordering of the industry. Certainly from the reader's perspective, the takeovers have resulted in fewer kinds of different books being published by the old-line houses. On the other hand, the new houses, unencumbered by layers of bureaucracy and accountability to a parent corporation, have been able to exercise the kind of flexibility and risk taking that have always been the hallmark of a successful publisher, in both cultural and financial terms.

Most readers are only dimly aware of what goes on in the book trade and generally have little concern for the success or failure of a particular publisher. Readers, naturally, are concerned with books and authors. While the mergers and takeovers of the last few decades have tended to restrict the variety and diversity of the kinds of books published by the old-line houses, this restriction has not been as severe as many critics have suggested. And counterbalancing this restriction has been the rise of the small houses that have more than made up for any lack by the old firms.

From the reader's perspective there is a greater diversity of books available, and indeed each year sees an increase in the overall number of titles published. However, while there is no literary crisis, we most certainly face a literacy crisis. In spite of the fact that more and more authors and books are published each year, how many people are reading them? It is estimated that as much as a third of the population of the United States is functionally illiterate, and many others, though literate, do not read books. Historically, we have made great progress in extending basic literacy to women in the late eighteenth and early nineteenth centuries, to African-Americans following Emancipation, and to newly arrived immigrants at the end of the nineteenth century and into the twentieth. While the newly literate citizen in the past would naturally turn to periodicals and books for information and entertainment, the advent of competing media such as radio and television has reduced the appeal of reading. If we believe with historian and former Librarian of Congress Daniel Boorstin that "our democracy is based on books and reading," and if we acknowledge that only half of our population consists of active readers, then we have great cause for concern for the future of our democratic nation. The community of the book—authors, editors, publishers, booksellers, librarians, wholesalers, literary agents, critics, reviewers, journalists, translators, educators, and readers— has been mobilized through the efforts and programs of a number of key governmental and private organizations (including the Center for the Book in the Library of Congress). These efforts have had a significant impact in promoting reading and literacy, particularly in schools and libraries, but ultimately if we are to remain a democratic nation of informed citizens, the value of reading must be inculcated in the home as parents pass on a lifelong love for reading and books to their children. As Boorstin notes, "We must raise a citizenry who are qualified to choose their experiences for themselves, from the books past and present, and so secure the independence that only the reader can enjoy."

If there is a "crisis of the book" that has permeated the general reader's consciousness, it has to do with the future of the book. There is a growing perception that the two thousand–year era of the physical book is coming to an end and some new form of electronic book will take its place. Certainly new modes for the presentation and manipulation of text are developing with amazing rapidity. Many reference books, such as encyclopedias, dictionaries, bibliographies, and the like, have

By the late 1950s and the early 1960s, paperbacks had become a major force in publishing. Titles were now issued in cloth and paper, and the trend was even toward first publication in paper alone. A paperback blockbuster bestseller was far more profitable than a much shorter run for a best-selling hardback edition. Joseph Heller's Catch-22, *though not a blockbuster, is a Dell paperback classic that has maintained consistent sales through numerous editions. Illustrated here are seven editions in chronological order (the first edition at the upper left).*

been issued in digitized form on CD-ROM, a mode that has many advantages for searching and organizing information over the traditional paper format. Libraries have tended to emphasize electronic and online resources, and recently some academic and scholarly periodicals have been issued in electronic format, which makes them more timely, an important consideration, especially in the sciences. Those who see the end of an era point to such developments as indications of the book's imminent replacement by some digital form. Certainly some kinds of books, such as reference works, will be published in electronic format and may cease to be published in a traditional book format altogether. But to suggest that this development marks the end of the book is very shortsighted. Historically such technological developments have tended to be complementary and not exclusionary. The cinema did not replace the book, nor did radio or television: all exist side by side in a dynamic relationship that now includes the new digital medium. Given the extraordinary history of the book in our culture and its ubiquity across the nation at all levels, it seems more than premature to announce the demise of the book. No one can know with certainty what the future holds, but if the past is a guide to the future, the book will be with us for many centuries to come. Thomas Jefferson's affirmation, "I cannot live without books," still rings true today.

Further Reading

Billington, James H. *Books and the World*. Washington, D.C.: Library of Congress, 1988.

Bonn, Thomas L. *Undercover: An Illustrated History of American Mass Market Paperbacks*. New York: Penguin Books, 1982.

Boorstin, Daniel J. *The Republic of Letters: Librarian of Congress Daniel J. Boorstin on Books, Reading, and Libraries, 1975–1987*. Washington, D.C.: Library of Congress, 1989.

Brown, Richard D. *Knowledge Is Power: The Diffusion of Information in Early America, 1700–1865*. Oxford: Oxford University Press, 1989.

Bruccoli, Matthew, ed. *The Profession of Authorship in America, 1800–1878*. Columbus: Ohio State University Press, 1968.

Charvat, William. *Literary Publishing in America, 1790–1850*. Philadelphia: University of Pennsylvania Press, 1959.

Cole, John Y. *Jefferson's Legacy: A Brief History of the Library of Congress*. Washington, D.C.: Library of Congress, 1993.

The Community of the Book: A Directory of Organizations and Programs, compiled by Maurvene D. Williams and edited by John Y. Cole. Washington, D.C.: Library of Congress, 1993.

Coser, Lewis A., Charles Kadushin, and Walter W. Powell. *Books: The Culture & Commerce of Publishing*. New York: Basic Books, 1982.

Davis, Kenneth C. *Two-Bit Culture: The Paperbacking of America*. Boston: Houghton Mifflin, 1984.

Hart, James D. *The Popular Book: A History of America's Literary Taste*. New York: Oxford University Press, 1950.

Lehman-Haupt, Hellmut. *The Book in America: A History of the Making and Selling of Books in the United States*. New York: R.R. Bowker, 1939, 1951.

Madison, Charles. *Book Publishing in America*. New York: McGraw-Hill, 1966.

Mott, Frank Luther. *Golden Multitudes: The Story of Best Sellers in the United States*. New York: Macmillan, 1947.

Sheehan, Donald. *This Was Publishing: A Chronicle of the Book Trade in the Gilded Age*. Bloomington: Indiana University Press, 1952.

Tanselle, G. Thomas. *Guide to the Study of United States Imprints*. Cambridge, Mass.: Belknap Press, 1971.

Tebbel, John. *Between the Covers: The Rise and Transformation of Book Publishing in America*. New York: Oxford University Press, 1987.

———. *A History of Book Publishing in the United States*. New York: R.R. Bowker, 1972–1981.

Thomas, Isaiah. *The History of Printing in America*. Worcester, Mass., 1810; Albany, N.Y.: Munsell, 1874; New York: Weathervane Books, 1970.

Wroth, Lawrence. *The Colonial Printer*. New York: Grolier Club, 1931; Portland, Maine: Southworth-Anthoensen Press, 1938.

Sources

Illustrations for this book come from various divisions within the Library of Congress. The Prints and Photographs Division (P&P) holds, among its millions of items, the following discrete collections, cites to which will be found on these pages: the Poster Collection (Pos), the New York World-Telegram & Sun Collection (NYWT&S), and material kept in "Lots" (Lot ___). Illustrations for this volume also were drawn from the Rare Book and Special Collections Division (RBD); the Manuscript Division (MSS); the Newspaper and Current Periodical collections (N&CP); the General Collections (Gen); the Publishing Office (Publ) and the Center for the Book (CFB).

Those who wish to order reproductions of illustrations in this book should contact the Library's Photoduplication Service and cite the Library of Congress negative numbers, or item call numbers provided below. *Please note:* Negative numbers begin with the following prefixes: LC-USZ62, LC-USZ61-, LC-C801-, LC-USZC2-(color), LC-USZC4-(color), US-BH-, US-D4-, US-F34-, LC-MSS (Manuscript Division negative). (Negatives held in the Rare Book and Special Collections Division will be indicated by "RBD neg.") All other numbers are call numbers for the books or other materials from which the illustration was taken; where these are not available, the abbreviation for the division holding the item is given. When multiple images appear on a page, negative numbers will be given in the order the images are arranged, left to right, top to bottom.

Chapter I: (7) BS1440 .B4 1640 [RBD] (RBD b/w neg. available for title page and 23d Psalm); (9, bottom), NYWT&S [P&P]; (11) LC-USZ62-3025; (12) BS345 .A2E4 1663 [RBD]; (14) BX7255 .M36W5 [RBD]; (15, bottom), PS711 .S4 1678 [RBD]; (17) NYWT&S [P&P]; (19) BX7676 .A2A4 [RBD]; (20) LC-USZ62-47651; (22) E302 .6 .F8 P6 [Gen]; (23) LC-USZ62-75475; (27) LC-USZ62-45280; (28) LC-USZ62-8238; (29) LC-USZ62-10658; (30) LC-USZ62-54126; (31) MSS; (32) RBD/PUBL, PUBL; (33) PUBL, LC-MSS-31021-44; (34) N&CP/PUBL; (35) JK154 1788 Copy 4 [RBD].

Chapter II: (39) F69 .M5 [RBD]; (40) PE1144 .W4 1790 [RBD]; (41) PZ6 .G639H [RBD (posed shot PUBL)]; (42) BS560 1788, p. 76 [RBD]; (43) BS185 1799 .W6 [RBD]; (44) PR3291 .A1A32 [RBD]; (46) LC-USZ62-28998; (48) AP2 .A2A8 Vol. 1 (1787) [RBD]; (50) G114 .G9 1794 Vol. 1

[RBD], QL50 .G62 1795, Vol. 2 [RBD, Toner Coll.]; (51) LC-USZ62-64499 (full encyclopedia page); (53) E312 .W37 [RBD].

Libraries in America: (56) LOT 12003, p. 15 [P&P], LC-D4-71172; (57) LC-C801-77; (58) LC-USZ62-22253; (60) LC-USF34-8833-D; (63) LC-D4-13257.

Chapter III: (64) LC-BH82-5244; (67) LC-BH8277-63; (68) PZ3 .C786L Vol. 1 [RBD], PS1608 .A2 1841 [RBD (posed shot, PUBL)]; (69) LC-USZ62-67575; (70) McGuffey Coll., No. 88 [RBD]; (73) LC-USZ62-54168; (74) E165 .D537 [RBD], E165 .D54 [RBD]; (76) BS185 1846 .N43 Vol. 1, p. 1 [RBD]; (77) NY Times 12/12/1853, Vol. III, No. 697 [N&CP], Z473 .H29A [Gen]; (78) E449 .D749 1849 [Gen]; (79) Broadside Coll., portfolio 186, No. 26 [RBD]; (80) PS2609 .A1 1845a [RBD]; (81) LC-BH82-4096, PS1868 .A1 1850 [RBD]; (82) LC-USZ62-11212, PS2954 .U5 1852d, Vol. 1 [RBD]; (83) LC-USZ62-90560 (title page), LC-USZ61-361 (Thoreau), LC-USZ62-90561 (map); (84) LC-USZ62-39759; (85) Dime Novel Coll. [RBD]; (87) F123 .H298 [RBD, Toner Coll.]; (88) LC-USZ62-11897 (Lincoln), LC-USZ62-68934 (girls).

Reading in America: (90) LC-C8101-119 (couple), LC-USZ62-111126 (boy on bench), LC-USF34-31187-D (girl); (91) LC-USF34-31170-D (sharecropper), LC-USF34-10825-D (Buckboard Charlie); (92) LC-USF33-16090-Ma (man on porch), PUBL/CFB (poster).

Chapter IV: (95) LC-USZ62-17966 (detail); (98) Z473 .H74 [RBD]; (99) LC-USZ62-60538 (Twain), LC-USZ62-52597 (title page); (100) PZ7 .A395 Do [RBD], Juvenile Coll., Alger [RBD]; (101) TX703 .S5 1808 [RBD], TX825 .F23 [Gen]; (102) LC-USZ62-71614, LC-MSS-18630-6; (103) LC-USZ62-47392, PZ3 .W768 V [RBD]; (104) LC-USZ62-42386, Gen/PUBL; (105) Dime Novel Coll. [RBD], Dime Novel Coll. [RBD]; (106) LC-USZ62-43648; (107) LC-USZ62-24871; (108) LC-USZ62-84696; (110) Z232 .D69D6 1913 [Gen]; (111) Seaside Library, Vol. 1xxvi, n. 1537 [RBD]; (112) Dime Novel Coll. [RBD]; (113) LC-USZC4-2262.

Books at War: (116) ASE Coll. [RBD]; (118) LC-USZ62-105281; (119) LC-USZ62-114275.

Chapter V: (120) Z473 .L5665 1970 [RBD]; (122) LC-USZ62-42536; (125) LC-USZ62-103661; (126) HV5275 .W15 1955 [Gen]; (128) RBD; (132) LC-USZ62-107991; (133) QH545 .P4 C38 1962 [RBD]; (134) TL240 .N25 [Gen], LC-U9-24801-3s; (136) PS3521 .E735 0534 1957 [RBD]; (137) PS3521 E735 D48 [RBD]; (140) Dell Paperback Coll. [RBD].

Afterword

he Center for the Book in the Library of Congress is pleased to have assisted in the publication of *The Book in America*. Encouraging the study of the history of books has been part of the center's program since it was established in 1977. At a planning meeting in April 1978, historian Elizabeth Eisenstein—who later served as the center's first visiting scholar—called on the center to sponsor projects that examined how the proliferation of printed materials had altered the traditional roles of the book and the printed word in our society. The activities to be examined, she noted, extended from authorship to reading, and encompassed printing, publishing, and the distribution of printed materials.

Since 1978, the history of the book has burgeoned as an interdisciplinary field of study, bringing social and intellectual history to bear on the printed artifact. The major impetus in the United States has been the American Antiquarian Society's Program in the History of the Book in American Culture. The Center for the Book, drawing on the rich and varied collections of the Library of Congress, makes its own distinctive contributions to book history.

Founded with the mandate to "stimulate public interest and research in the role of the book in the diffusion of knowledge," the center has pursued this broad goal through symposia and lectures; reading and literacy projects in schools and libraries; television and radio announcements promoting writers and their writing; traveling exhibitions; special events; a visiting scholar program; and the publication of more than fifty pamphlets and books—including *The History of Books: A Guide to Selected Resources in the Library of Congress*, by Alice D. Schreyer (1987). Pioneering conferences sponsored by the center have included "Literacy in Historical Perspective" (1980); "Images of the World: the Atlas Through History" (1984); "Getting the Books Out: The Book in 19th-Century America" (1985); "Publishing and Readership in Revolutionary France and America" (1989); "The Book in the Islamic World" (1990); and "The Hebrew Book" (1991). In 1994, the center hosted the annual meeting of the Society for the History of Authorship, Reading, and Publishing (SHARP), and it continues to encourage the growth of state and regional book history centers throughout the country.

In its advocacy of books, reading, and libraries the center has been aided by a powerful and widespread network of reading promotion partners that now includes thirty affiliated state centers and more than one hundred national civic and educational organizations. This is potent testament, indeed, to the crucial importance books, literacy and the life of the mind have played, and continue to play, in the evolution of American society. James Madison, for whom the third, and largest, Library of Congress building is named, expressed this well when he wrote this cogent—and cautionary—observation in 1822: "Knowledge will forever govern ignorance: And a people who mean to be their own governours, must arm themselves with the power which knowledge gives." Richard Clement's thoughtful overview of *The Book in America* reminds us how pertinent that observation has remained throughout the many sweeping changes history has brought us.

John Y. Cole, Director
The Center for the Book

Index